KIDDERMINSTER
AND DISTRICT
IN THE SECOND WORLD WAR

Recollections from the Home Front

Edited by
BILL WOOD, BOB MILLWARD and ROBERT BARBER

for the Kidderminster and District
Archaeological and Historical Society

SUTTON PUBLISHING

Sutton Publishing Limited
Phoenix Mill · Thrupp · Stroud
Gloucestershire · GL5 2BU

First published 2006

Copyright © Kidderminster and
District Archaeological and
Historical Society, 2006

**British Library Cataloguing in Publication
Data**
A catalogue record for this book is available from
the British Library.

ISBN 0-7509-4551-6

Typeset in 10.5/13.5 Plantin.
Typesetting and origination by
Sutton Publishing Limited.
Printed and bound in England by
J.H. Haynes & Co. Ltd, Sparkford.

*Kidderminster and District
Archaeological and Historical
Society*

Kidderminster and District Archaeological and Historical Society celebrates its fiftieth anniversary in 2007. The society meets at 7.30 p.m. every first, second, fourth and fifth Wednesday in the month between October and April at St George's Church Annexe, Radford Avenue, Kidderminster, for lectures and discussions. The programme for each season is published on the society website: www.communigate.co.uk/worcs/kidderminsterhistorysoc. Visitors are welcome for a small fee.

CONTENTS

Victory celebration party in Clarence Street, a joint event with nearby Leswell Street. Tulips on the table indicate that this was a VE party. Participants include Robert Anderson, May Batchelor, Roy Baynton, Robina Burford, Peter Conway, Margaret Dixon, Dulcie Edge, Paddy Evans, Michael Everley, David Gwilliam, Ron Jones, Pat Lythall, Ann McGilvray, Joyce Owen, Cyril Parker, John Parker, Michael Parker, Ann Potts, Muriel Potts, Graham Price, Sheila Price, Stella Price, Carol Pugh, Christine Reynolds, Pamela Rowley, Pam Simmonds, Valerie Simmonds, Bertie Teague, Patricia Wanklin. (*Godfrey Jones*)

FOREWORD

Much has been written about the Second World War, about the armed services, politicians and our major cities, but little has been done to record the effects of the war on ordinary people left at home living in areas designated as safe. This book is a timely record from the memories of ordinary people in the Kidderminster area who contributed to the war effort and lived through the great changes that were enforced on everyone.

I was not brought up in Kidderminster, but in an even safer area on the edge of the Yorkshire Dales. My father was too old for call-up and so became the village Air Raid Precautions warden. I envied his tin helmet and proper gas mask with separate eye-pieces. Mine, which was always with me in its cardboard box at home or at school, was a crude, ungainly device with a screen for both eyes – far inferior, I thought!

We were spared the horrors of bombing in our immediate neighbourhood and the nearest I got to the Blitz was while staying with friends near Liverpool when the noise of the bombs and anti-aircraft fire was terrifying even at some distance.

I remember how hard my mother slaved to keep our clothes presentable, how socks were continually darned and clothes enlarged. I remember the hard labour involved in keeping hens and pigs and growing vegetables and fruit to supplement our own and our neighbours' rations.

I still have my aircraft recognition silhouettes and a few precious pre-war treasures. During the war toys, understandably, disappeared from the shops – even if, because of strict petrol rationing, you could get to them.

I also recall vividly the day when pit props arrived to strengthen our cellar roof to make an air-raid shelter. At the height of the fear of invasion signposts were removed and my parents made preparations to remove to an isolated shepherd's hut well off the beaten track.

My memories are trivial compared with those people directly affected by the war, but I look forward to reading this book to learn of others' experiences and to revive memories. The Kidderminster & District Archaeological & Historical Society has performed a valuable service in producing a unique record of life during those extraordinary years.

Dr Richard Taylor, MP

ACKNOWLEDGEMENTS

The authors and the Kidderminster & District Archaeological & Historical Society are grateful for the time and trouble taken by so many people to provide anecdotes and reminiscences about the war years, and also for the many photographs, souvenirs and memorabilia made available. Sincere thanks are therefore given to:

Raymond Badger
Vera Badger
Robert Barber
Roger Baulk
Jackie Bayliss
Roy Bayliss
William Bradley
Sally Brown
Robina Burford
Leonard Burrows
Bill Bury
Peter Carter
Doug Chamberlin
The late Michael
    Compton
Bill Connolly
John Connolly
Jeff Cooper
Janet Cowburn
Mike Cowburn
John Davis
Sally Dickson
Graham Dowe
June Dowe
Graham Edginton
Maurice Fallon
Hazel Fallon
Stella Field

Edna Fletcher
Judy George
Jennifer Gowland
Catherine Guest
Edwina Guest
Peggy Guest
Daisy Harris
Bill Harrison
Mrs S. Healey
Monica Hill
Mary Hoban
Betty Hodges
Jill Jackson
Patricia James
Godfrey Jones
Geoff Jukes
Sheila Kirk
Maureen Lawrence
Les Lench
Keith Lloyd
Jessie Maskell
John Melloy
Pam Melloy
Beryl Millichap
Phillip Millward
Alf Mole
Anne Mole
Eric Mole

Cyril Moore
Brian Pearsall
Margaret Phelan
Joan Phipps
Marjorie Rivers
Cynthia Rogers
Ken Rudd
Ruth Rudd
John Russell
Norman Ryder
Mrs Sewell
Mervyn Silcox
Patti Silk
Brian Stephens
Betty Sutton
Fred Sutton
Jeremy Thomas
Melvyn Thompson
Bryan Tolley
Pam Upsall
Les Wicks
Mick Wilkes
Mrs D.E. Williams
Graham Williams
Bob Worboys
Valerie Yapp
Jack Young

We also thank others who wish to remain anonymous. Our profuse apologies if we have inadvertently missed anyone from this list.

We are grateful to the following sources of information: the Worcester City Museum & Art Gallery for providing and giving permission to use the photograph of the Mickey Mouse gas mask; Martin Garnett of the Imperial War Museum for information about German Second World War incendiary bombs; the Bodleian Library, University of Oxford, for permitting us to use a photograph of the cover for *Instructions for American Servicemen in Britain*. We appreciate access to photographs and information about Brintons' and Tomkinsons' factories during the Second World War in the Archive Collection of The Carpet Museum and our thanks are due to Kidderminster Library for allowing use of documents and photographs from their Home Guard collection, and for other facilities. The availability of the records at Worcester Record Office has been much valued, as has the information gathered at the Britain at War Experience exhibition, London, 2005. The aerial reconnaissance photograph near Bewdley is by kind permission of Messrs A. and N. Turley/US National Archives. The Robert Opie Collection kindly allowed us to reproduce the advertisement for a leg dye.

We offer our grateful thanks to Home Front Recall for providing a grant without which this publication could not have been produced in its present form.

We owe a special thank you to Pam Melloy, now of Queensland, Australia. Pam's enquiry to this society about the bomb raid which left a crater next to her house in Sutton Park Road, and the subsequent information provided by her, initiated the 'twinkle in the eye' that led to this book.

The editors would like to put on record their deep gratitude for the support and understanding shown by their wives during the protracted time spent preparing this publication.

INTRODUCTION

The effects of the Second World War were felt in every city, town and village in the land, but the way in which ordinary people who were not engaged in the actual fighting went about their business and had their lives disrupted has not so far been set down for the Kidderminster area.

The district was officially designated a safe area but, nevertheless, life changed considerably. The world-renowned carpet industry was put on hold; munitions and war work replaced conventional occupations in and around the town. Food and clothing shortages had to be dealt with, and precautions taken against air raids and invasion. Evacuees took over parts of some schools and there was a huge influx of military personnel. Seaside holidays, street lighting, liquor and dining out became matters of memory for many; and children were born who reached school age without ever experiencing such things as new toys.

Apart from the newspapers, heavily censored at the time, there has been little formal recording of life in the Kidderminster area during the period 1939–45. A wealth of information exists in the memories of those alive at the time and it was felt to be important to record this valuable archive material as soon as possible. The purpose of this book, which has been prepared by Kidderminster & District Archaeological & Historical Society, is therefore to capture the oral history of the war years as related by these people and set it out in an appropriate context to form a picture of life in those dark days. This will provide future generations with a more intimate knowledge of the period than could be gained from conventional historical sources, and at the same time rekindle many memories of those who lived through the Second World War.

Inevitably, after so much time has elapsed, the detail of recollected events will differ from person to person and from official accounts or newspaper reports. Yet we hope that we have captured the flavour of those times – if not always strict historical accuracy.

Money Then and Now

The value of money has changed significantly since the war years. Taking the Retail Price Index as a measure, £1 in 1942 was worth the equivalent of about £31 in 2005.

Coinage also changed with decimalisation on 10 February 1971. The equivalent values are shown below:

New	Old
5p	1*s*
12.5p	2*s* 6*d* ('half crown')
0.1p	¼*d* ('farthing')

Children, evacuated from Birmingham to Kidderminster, wearing gas masks. *(Sheila Kirk)*

I
EVACUEES

Many people still have recollections of evacuees staying in the area around Kidderminster. The concept of evacuation was to move children, mothers and disabled people away from areas of high risk. Throughout Britain just under one and a half million people were evacuated; over 827,000 children, 524,000 mothers, a further 13,000 expectant mothers, 7,000 disabled people and 103,000 teachers and helpers.

Before the outbreak of war on 3 September 1939 the government had decided that certain 'safe areas' were less likely to be subjected to enemy attack. The Kidderminster locality obviously fell into this category as it received many hundreds of evacuees. Industrial Birmingham was a prime target for bombing and the majority of people evacuated to the Kidderminster region were from in and around Birmingham. Others were from Stafford and Coventry – and one school from Clacton-on-Sea came later in the war.

Clearly the Prime Minister's family thought this area was safe. One contributor tells us: 'as soon as war was declared Neville Chamberlain's grandchildren, by his daughter Diane, were temporarily evacuated from Birmingham to the home of their nurse's parents at Eymore'.

Kidderminster and district had been identified as a reception area for evacuation of schoolchildren from Smethwick. Schools charged with hosting these children started the term one week late, on 11 September, allowing teachers to help with billeting arrangements. Many children had arrived in the town as early as 1 September. The *Kidderminster Shuttle*, 16 September, reported:

The evacuees from Smethwick who are billeted in the town are receiving systematic instruction under their own teachers at various centres. St George's Mixed (Junior) School – 35 children from the top stream of Brass House Lane; Coventry St Boys' School – 31 children from the 2nd stream department and Coventry St Girls' School – 31 children from the bottom stream. St George's Infants has 70 children from Brass House Lane.

Other centres used were: Franche Church Hall – 63 junior children from Crockett's Lane; the School of Science – 74 senior boys and 62 senior girls; Bennett St Infants – 48 infants. Holy Innocents Hall was also used. About 500 evacuee children attended school that week in the town.

Alf Mole recalls evacuees being billeted in Lorne Street and Lea Street. 'They walked up the slope in great crocodiles from Kidderminster station.'

Evacuees stayed with local families who were required to accept at least one person if they had sufficient room. Civilian billeting officers directed evacuees to specific houses and many families suddenly found an increase in the numbers living in their homes. It could not have been easy as the allowance for taking in a refugee was fairly meagre: 10*s* per child or, if more than one child was taken, the payment was 8*s* 6*d* each. The intention was that evacuee families should be billeted together. This was not always possible and splitting up of mothers and children or brothers and sisters could lead to a great deal of additional unhappiness.

Mostly it was children who were evacuated to this area. Roy Bayliss remembers it well: 'The evacuees came to Areley Kings in a charabanc and disembarked at the Parish Rooms. They went behind the railings and leaned against the wall or sat on their little suitcases waiting to be claimed. Later I struck up a friendship with a little girl that lasted for several years. At the end of the war she returned to Birmingham and I heard recently that she is now a very sick lady – I wrote to her at Christmas.'

The Carter family of Larches Road with their evacuee, Marion Tillison, standing in front of the group. From left: Reg Carter, Peter Carter, John Carter, Monica Carter and Nell Carter. *(Monica Hill)*

Jackie Bayliss had first-hand experience of an evacuee living in their house.

Joan was a bit older than my sister and I. She must have worried about bombing because one day, when my mum came back from the shop, Joan had put us under the table. She was practising drill for if there was an air raid. When she came to us from Smethwick she had nothing but the clothes she stood up in and the first thing my mum did was to ask the landlady at The Squirrel, Mrs Sutton, if she had any of her daughter's old clothes to spare. We heard nothing from her after the war when she went back home.

Monica Hill and her brother Peter Carter recall that within the first week of war starting they had their first evacuee. Marion Tillison was part of the contingent of Smethwick schoolchildren allocated to Foley Park, and she quickly became part of the family.

The silly thing was the war wasn't really happening in Birmingham then; we even went there once or twice at weekends. She stayed a few months but, because all was quiet, she went back home. We kept in touch for a long time until after she was married. Later we had a very, very nice boy called John Storr who went to Hartlebury Grammar School. He had been evacuated from Birmingham to Hartlebury. His room was needed for family who had been displaced and Peter came home saying that there was this boy who needed help. John later went to Canada and whenever he comes home I'm part of the family he visits.

At the outbreak of war Betty Hodges (née Harrison), aged 6, was evacuated to Newport, Shropshire, but soon returned home because nothing happened:

When the bombs did start dropping I was evacuated to Kidderminster with my younger brother Bill – but to different addresses. We came by charabancs run by Nash's. I first stayed with a nice family called Ball who lived in a terraced house named Engadine opposite St George's Park, Radford Avenue. I was taken to concerts, in which their daughter Dawn was dancing, at the town hall and at the workhouse. Then, for a short time, I was at a house near the sugar beet factory before moving on to Bewdley to Herne's Nest, off Park Lane, a large house with old servants' quarters and service bells. There were other girls from all over the country and I was friendly with a girl from London. I was taken to visit her in hospital when she became ill; but she died. My school was in Lax Lane.

Marjorie Rivers lived at Shatterford. 'They used to come round and see where they could put evacuees. Mrs Marks down the lane had two girls from London. The attitude to evacuees was tolerant rather than welcoming.'

A Stourport resident recalls:

We had two evacuees in our house at Abberley. Barbara Phillips was a sweet little girl from Birmingham who brought her belongings in a brown paper bag. I don't think she'd had a very good upbringing and she didn't stay long. We kept in touch with Barbara until early this year when her husband replied to an invitation to my mother's 90th birthday saying she had died recently. Edith Hawkins was an evacuee from London and part of the Grove School; they all seemed quite upper-class. The Scout Hut was used as their school and Edith then went to Abberley school until she passed the 11+. We are still in touch [2005]; we exchange cards at Christmas and she visited us for a family celebration.

Melvyn Thompson's mother took evacuees: 'Our semi-detached house had three bedrooms and my brother and I shared. For most of the time our box room was occupied by Miss Tugwell who worked for the Pay Corps at Pike Mills. After the war she used to write to my mother from her home in Ramsgate. At one stage we were sent two evacuees from Smethwick. The boy was called Derek but I can't remember his sister's name. My mother says that the first thing she had to do was to put them in the bath and scrub them clean.'

Sheila Kirk found in an old box of her mother's a photograph of two children wearing gas masks (see page x). 'I remember, when I was 6 or 7 years old, playing with these children who I think were evacuees staying near my home in Bruce Road: the names Bobby and Pat spring to mind. They came from Birmingham way, with broad accents we could hardly understand. I cannot be certain whether they were related to each other, or how long they stayed.'

Les Wicks from Hammersmith was 8 years old in the summer of 1940 when he was evacuated from London to Sutton Park Road, Kidderminster, with his bedridden grandmother.

I think Granny was in the Workhouse Infirmary. The first time I visited her I walked through a park and picked some flowers; I got told off by Granny for that. Once I wondered what some boys were doing lighting a fire by the canal and discovered they were smoking out a wasps' nest. I probably beat the Olympic sprint record getting home, only to get covered in blue (from the blue bags used in washing) to treat the stings.

The woman I was billeted with had a 13-year-old son and a married daughter. I used to go for Saturday morning baths in the daughter's council house. I spent a lot of time in the park opposite the house and used to play on an old First World War tank. I learned to read in the kitchen with a

Hotspur comic; that was a wonderful feeling! I constantly ran errands to the Co-op a few yards up the road from where we lived.

I missed my Mum and Dad and was a bit unhappy living in limbo, wishing for when I could go home. My mother came to see me more than once, but I can only remember when she and my aunt brought me a bike and taught me to ride. When I eventually went home nobody could understand my Midlands accent!

Les recently visited Kidderminster with some of his family to relive old memories. His little grandson's next homework diary included: 'I went to Kidderminster to see where my Grandad was sent to be safe during the war.'

Most evacuees found the town and countryside around Kidderminster strange after what they had been used to – but one or two made their homes in the area. Maurice Fallon was one.

I came as an evacuee from Moseley Grammar School in 1940. There were 150 of us and we should have gone to King Charles School, but as it was already full we had lessons in the headmaster's house and assemblies in St John's Centre. We were largely taught by our own teachers who came with us. I was one of only two boys studying woodworking and engineering drawing and these weren't catered for in Kidderminster, so every week we had a master come from our school in Moseley to teach us.

I was one of those compulsorily placed in families and, first of all, I lodged with a very well off family in St John's Avenue. A teenage boy was possibly not an ideal lodger and when the lady of the house became pregnant I was moved to Greatfield Road. Teenage girls took my place – probably they would have been more useful helping with the baby. When I moved I took my ration book with me which was needed to get the food to feed me. After leaving school I got a job in local munitions and was deferred until I was 21. By this time the war was over – but I was still called up and served in the Pay Corps. However, I had met my future wife at work and came back here to live afterwards.

Another evacuee who returned to the area was Mary Hoban. 'I came to Areley Kings as an evacuee after being bombed out three times in Birmingham. It was a complete contrast to where I had lived before. I returned to Birmingham and eventually got married. Some time later my brother bought a house in Areley Kings because he liked the fishing near there. Our house in Birmingham was too large so I asked him to look out for a house near to his. He found one – and it turned out to be the same house where I had lived as an evacuee. We moved into the house and so I have lived in that house twice. The family who owned it had been decorators but the house hadn't been altered in the years since I had lived there previously.'

One evacuee to Wolverley from Smethwick has only good memories about those times:

One day whilst Mother was at work she heard the list of schools that were to be evacuated from the Birmingham area. This was about ten days before the formal declaration of war. She went straight to Uplands School, where my elder sister and I were pupils, and was given a list of items to purchase for when we were evacuated. She and Father went to the central warehouse in Birmingham Bull Ring and got exactly what was on the list for each of us – including a mackintosh, gymslip, two liberty bodices, a haversack and labels for our clothes.

We gathered at school on Friday 1 September 1939 and were taken by bus to Smethwick Junction Station and from there to Bewdley. My sister and I recognised Bewdley as we had been there for a short holiday in a chalet in Northolt Lane by the river. A fleet of buses waited to take the various schools from Smethwick to different destinations. Uplands School went to Wolverley, Crockett's Lane School to Franche and I can't remember where Holly Lodge High School went.

On arrival at Wolverley School we walked up the slope and across the playground to the assembly hall. We were given a bag containing rations including condensed milk, corned beef, a small tin of Bournvita. We formed a queue to meet the villagers we were to stay with, and my sister and I were last. There were only two ladies left when it was our turn; one said she could take only one evacuee. The other said she had room for four and so we went with her as Mother had insisted that we shouldn't be parted. Thus we arrived to stay with 'Auntie May and Uncle Ewart' who treated us as their nieces.

The next day the air-raid siren went and we rushed down into the cellar, put on our gas masks and blocked up the cellar grating. It was silent outside apart from the cows mooing in the fields, so we soon abandoned the cellar. Auntie had posted a letter straight away to my parents on the Friday and they arrived to see us on the Sunday morning in their neighbours' car. They found that us girls had gone to Worcester in Uncle's car. It was a luxury for us as our family didn't own one. However, Mother and Father visited us each Saturday at Wolverley.

So began a long and happy time at Wolverley – we truly hardly knew there was a war on. Auntie and Uncle were grocers; we wanted for nothing and were extremely well looked after. The period was a tremendously defining influence on my life.

Many evacuees went home after a few months but more came later when the bombing of Birmingham started. Clacton High School came a year later and we had Ruth and Vera staying with us. At Blakeshall Hall, Mrs Graham made up a nursery for the toddlers she was expecting but was surprised to get some tall sixth formers billeted on her! My sister returned home after five years but I stayed on to complete my education at Kidderminster High School for girls.

In August 1944 another smaller wave of evacuees came to Kidderminster because of the flying bomb attacks on London and the south-east. The last at St George's Infant School returned home in June 1945.

The reminiscences of fourteen children evacuated from Smethwick to Kidderminster, Stourport, Bewdley and surrounding areas have been published by the Smethwick Heritage Centre Trust. Recollections are mixed. One boy thought he had been lucky to have lived with such kind people and believes that his hosts saved his life by providing nourishment that he had previously lacked. However, another found that pocket money provided by her parents was taken to 'put into savings'. The savings were never seen again. Harry Boughton and his brother stayed with a Mrs Davies who ran a shop that sold sweets in Coventry Street. They were trusted to pay for sweets that they ate, but instituted what was probably the first 'Buy one, get one free' scheme.

To conclude this chapter we refer to the Kidderminster Town Council Minutes for 29 May 1940, where a sequel to the evacuation of Smethwick children to the town is recorded:

Gift of Books – Smethwick Corporation. The Chairman reported that in addition to several other gifts received, for which the donors had been thanked by the Committee, the Corporation of Smethwick had presented to the Library 130 new non-fiction children's books in recognition of the library facilities granted to children evacuated from Smethwick.

Moved by Councillor Talbot, seconded by Alderman Davies, and Resolved, 'that the Town Council expresses its sincere thanks to the Mayor and Corporation of Smethwick for their generous gift'.

2
AIR-RAID PRECAUTIONS

As early as 1937 the government clearly thought that the possibility of war with Germany should be taken seriously. Following the Air Raid Precautions Act in that year, advisory and instructional booklets were issued on topics such as *The Protection of Your Home Against Air Raids* and *Some Things You Should Know If War Should Come*. Attempting to alleviate undue concern, the Home Office stressed: 'The need for them is not related to any belief that war is imminent. It arises from the fact that the risk from attack from the air, however remote, is a risk that cannot be ignored.'

We know from a poster published locally that recruiting for the infant ARP services began in Kidderminster in October 1938; all you had to do was complete the application form.

BOROUGH OF KIDDERMINSTER
A. R. P.
RECRUITING CAMPAIGN

In connect ion with the National Recruiting Campaign for the enrolment of 1,000,000 Volunteers for Air Raid Precautions Services, MEETINGS and DEMONSTRATIONS will take place in the Borough as follows:-

THURSDAY, 6TH OCTOBER, 1938
WOMEN'S DAY.
Women Volunteers are urgently needed and a Meeting will take place in the TOWN HALL, KIDDERMINSTER, at 8 P.M. on the above date, presided over by **THE DEPUTY MAYOR** (Councillor E. C. Addenbrooke, J.P.) when the necessity for Air Raid Precautions will be explained.

ALL WOMEN ARE INVITED
and enrolment forms will be available at the Meeting.

FRIDAY, 7th OCTOBER, 1938

A **PROCESSION** of the Air Raid Precautions Services will take place at 7-30 P.M. and will pass through the centre streets of the town.

AN APPEAL WILL BE MADE FROM THE TOWN HALL
FOR VOLUNTEERS

SATURDAY, 8TH OCTOBER, 1938

SPEECHES will be made at the Football Ground and Cinemas calling for Volunteers.

GAS-PROOF DEMONSTRATION ROOM
Open 3rd OCTOBER to 15th OCTOBER, 1938, inclusive

A room has been fitted up at No. 25 WORCESTER STREET showing the method of making a room gas-proof and the public are invited to visit this room, where information and advice will be given on the means available for protection against gas.

TIMES OF OPENING:

Mondays 7 p.m. to 9 p.m.	Thursdays 11 a.m. to 12-30 p.m. & 7 p.m. to 9 p.m.
Tuesdays 7 p.m. to 9 p.m.	Fridays 7 p.m. to 9 p.m.
Wednesdays 3 p.m. to 5 p.m.	Saturdays 2-30 p.m. to 4-30 p.m. & 7 p.m. to 9 p.m.

YOUR HELP IS NEEDED !   *ENROL NOW !!*

G. T. Cheshire & Sons Ltd., Coventry Street, Kidderminster

WORCESTERSHIRE COUNTY COUNCIL
AIR RAID PRECAUTIONS.

APPLICATION FORM.

I AM WILLING TO VOLUNTEER FOR:—
(Strike out headings that do not apply)

First Aid Service
Duties with Decontamination Parties
Duties with Rescue and Demolition Parties*
Service as Air Raid Warden
Service as Messenger with {Motor Cycle / Cycle
Service as Emergency Transport Driver with my {Car / Van / Lorry
Service as Auxiliary Fireman
* Work suitable for men employed in the building and allied trades.

Signature..

Address ....

An application form for volunteers to join various ARP services. (*Godfrey Jones*)

Left: A Kidderminster ARP recruiting campaign poster, 1938. (*Godfrey Jones*)

A.R.P.

HOME OFFICE
SCOTTISH OFFICE
MARCH · · · 1938

AIR RAID PRECAUTIONS

WHAT YOU CAN DO

THIS leaflet sets out the choices open to every British citizen who wishes to take his or her part in the voluntary national organisation of the Air Raid Precautions Services.

As the Home Secretary said in his broadcast speech on the 14th March, 1938, "If the emergency arose, I know you would come in your hundreds of thousands. But you would come untrained. For the work we may have to do one man trained beforehand is worth two or three who come at the last moment. We want at least a million men and women, and we want them for work that in an emergency would be exacting and dangerous. The job is not an amusement in peace-time, nor would it be a soft job in time of war. It is a serious job for free men and women who care for their fellows and for their Country."

The duties described here are mainly for what has been called passive defence. Young men preferring to take part in the active defence of their country can enlist either in the Territorial Army (which provides the Anti-Aircraft Units for the Home Defence) or in the Auxiliary Air Force; or in the Royal Navy (including the Royal Naval Volunteer Reserve) or Royal Marines, or the

Army (including the Supplementary Reserve), or the Royal Air Force (including the R.A.F. Volunteer Reserve). Particulars may be obtained from the local Recruiting Offices.

The police reserve and air raid precautions services described below do not admit men under 25, or in many cases under 30. Men over these ages, and in many cases women, can perform these duties.

PART 1—AIR RAID PRECAUTIONS SERVICES

Enrolment and Training.

Air raid precautions services are organised by the local authorities, and those wishing to volunteer should apply to the local Council Offices: or in the case of the auxiliary fire service and the fire brigade reserve, to the fire brigade station.

All training is provided free.

The more persons there are who are trained and know what to do for themselves and others, the better the country will be prepared. Those who are ready to perform duty, whether whole-time or part-time, in war will be enrolled in the appropriate service. But reserves will be necessary, and those who wish to have training in any of the duties described here, in case they would be available in time of war, can apply.

Pre-war issue of the booklet *Air Raid Precautions – What You Can Do*, March 1938. (*John Russell*)

John Russell was a head ARP warden in Kidderminster and preserved many of the training and advice booklets that were issued locally. One item, from March 1938, concerns *Air Raid Precautions – What You Can Do* and a second, *Training of Air Raid Wardens* (1939), cost 2d.

❖ ❖ ❖

In 1939 street lighting in the town was fuelled by coke gas. Most of the street lamps were disabled and a 'blackout' implemented. Bill Bury, who lived in Long Acre, recalls: 'Total blackout was the order of the day; all windows were fitted with thick, dark material. My father constructed outside shutters to close nightly.' Melvyn Thompson's father fitted wooden frames covered with old wallpaper inside the windows to prevent light escaping.

But perhaps the blackout was not completely universal, for it seems that some, but sparse, street lighting was allowed under controlled circumstances in critical areas of town. Maurice Fallon, as a teenager, was part of the police messenger service in Kidderminster. Cycling, essential for this work, was difficult as 'Street lamps were restricted and those left on were heavily shaded downward projecting lights. There would be one at a road junction and usually the next light was over 100 yards away.'

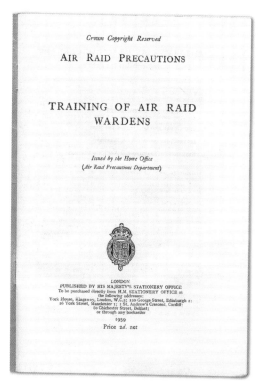

Pre-war issue of the booklet *Training of Air Raid Wardens*, 1939. (*John Russell*)

Nevertheless, most streets were very dark at night and breaking the blackout rule was an offence; police and air-raid wardens enforced the light ban. Anyone venturing out at night required a specially adapted low-light torch, as described by Alf Mole. 'The torches had a little slit cover, and on a pitch-black night you didn't know whether to have the strip of light longways or sideways; it was easy to miss kerbs.' To help night-time mobility pavement edges, tree trunks, doorways and other obstacles were often painted with white bands to make them more visible. Headlights on the few vehicles around had 'masks' fitted. Margaret Phelan describes a modified car headlight in some detail: 'The lower half of the reflector and the top half of the glass were painted black so that what little light came out pointed downwards – just enough for a driver going slowly.'

One warden took vehicle lighting instructions very seriously, according to Roy Bayliss. 'The man in charge of the ARP in Areley Kings was Mr Dilworth Lloyd, who lived in Areley Woods. His HQ was Kingston House – next door to the vet's. He was so conscientious that he refused to use lights on his car at all. One night he misjudged the turning from Dunley Road into Areley Lane. He crashed through the hedge and did a lot of damage to the car and himself.'

ARP wardens were at the heart of air-raid protection, providing a service that, as well as blackout duties, included general patrols, training, advice and testing of protection equipment such as gas masks. Central training was provided at the ARP school, Fairfield, Gloucestershire, to give local instructors the expertise for preparing groups in their areas. Film shows were held on some Sundays at the Central ABC Cinema in Oxford Street. Of course, many other services were closely involved with protecting the populace from the threat from the air: firewatchers, firemen, the police, the government, local authorities and, last but not least, individuals all had their own areas of responsibility.

The ARP warden system was organised into sectors covering different parts of the town. John Russell was head warden of C-sector, based in the cellars under the offices of Hepworths chemical factory in Coventry Street, conveniently next door to his wireless and cycle shop.

E-sector was nearby in South Street, next to St Andrew's (Tin) Church. We have heard of other units based in the fish shop near the Chester Tavern, Lorne Street; the Larches Road Club House; the cellar of the Sutton Arms, Sutton Park Road; and in Kidderminster station yard.

Individuals associated with the various groups, at one particular time, are shown in the table on page 12. It is not known for what purpose this information was used.

ARP wardens wore uniforms, armbands, lapel badges and sometimes a 'tin' helmet; they carried an ARP identity card and a whistle. Some groups were issued with a gas testing kit in case of gas attacks.

ARP warden's lapel badge. *(John Russell)*

Headquarters of C-Sector ARP group in the cellar under the offices of Hepworths Chemical Factory in Coventry Street. John Russell, wearing a beret, is with another warden, G.M. Jones. Note the standard issue steel hat hanging on the wall. *(John Russell)*

Table 1. *ARP warden membership sometime during the Second World War*

Sector	Incident Officers	Reception Officers
B	H. Cook, 105 Wolverhampton Road	W. Spencer, 166 Stourbridge Road F. Turner, 26 Wolverhampton Road
C	R.E. Foster, 47 Radford Avenue R. Williams, 64 Shrubbery Street	
D	H. Maund, 328 Hurcott Road M. Williams, 71 Bruce Road	R. Lylie, 3 James Road H. Curtis, 70 Hurcott Road
E	W. Hodges, 11 Cross Street J. Berry, 22 Bromsgrove Street	
F	H. Cane, 22 Comberton Hill E. Guest, Cherry Orchard	
G	C.E. Pagett, Chadstone, Comberton F.E. Dobson, 32 Chaddesley Road	
H	W.H. Lloyd, 77 Chester Road South G.F. Astle, 523 Chester Road South	Mr Price, Vicarage Crescent
J	F. Churchett, Larches Road S.J. Dex, 43 Aggborough Crescent	
L	H. Vale, 148 Sutton Road C.W. Cowley, 24 Poplar Road	
M	C.W. Hopkins, 31 Manor Avenue J. Hall, 144 Bewdley Hill	A.E. Gill, 149 Bewdley Hill J. Bedford, 28 Cobden Street
N	J. Turton, 10 Bennett Street	R. Robinson, 54 Franche Road J. McGilvray, 35 Marlpool Place

Other names submitted but did not attend.

A	J. Haden and S. Smith
B	L. Preece
N	F. Hay

Two types of armband used by ARP Wardens. *(John Russell)*

Worcestershire County Council

AIR RAID PRECAUTIONS

This is to certify that the Bearer

....

has been appointed as an Air Raid Warden. This is his authority to carry out the duties laid upon Wardens by the County Council of Worcestershire.

....

 -Town Clerk, Clerk.

....

Date of issue of card.........................

Date of appointment
of Warden.   ....

Signature of Warden.........................

F1353

ID card for ARP wardens. *(John Russell)*

Whistle issued to ARP
wardens. *(John Russell)*

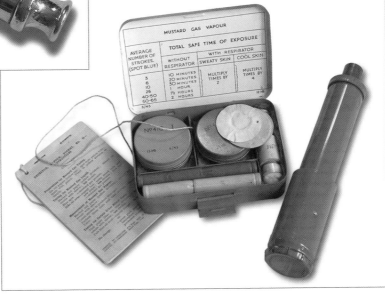

Gas-testing kit issued to ARP
units in case of gas attacks
from the air. *(John Russell)*

Training of their own members, other officials and the general public was a significant part of senior wardens' duties and in this they were helped by publications provided by government agencies.

The booklet *Air Raid Precautions Handbook No. 14 – The Fire Guards Handbook*, published in 1942, includes guidance on 'how to drop from upstairs windows', 'how to use a stirrup pump for tackling incendiary bombs indoors' and how to deal with an incendiary bomb in the street.

Much time was spent on routine administration. One of the logbooks for E-sector has survived among John Russell's memorabilia. It contains a wealth of minutiae concerning the organisation of the service: warden sheet returns, subsistence allowances, whether Post Warden Blencowe could play in the Chief's darts team against L-sector on Wednesday, and duty rotas. The latter was often a matter of contention and there was clearly some friction between paid and voluntary staff:

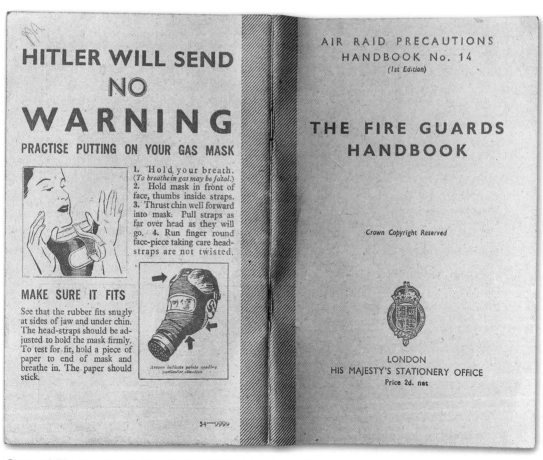

Cover of *The Fire Guards Handbook* published in 1942. (*John Russell*)

Extract from *The Fire Guards Handbook*: escaping from an upstairs window. *(John Russell)*

8 Dec 1942, 22.00hrs: Warden Hodges reported a difference of opinion with Voluntary Wardens about the manning of night duty; the arrangements made the previous night between Head Warden and Warden Davies not being agreeable to the latter.

22.05hrs: Wardens Davies, Dance and Roberts came into Post and after a discussion on the various issues at stake, including the distasteful subject of bickering at *paid Wardens*, the Head Warden offered to accept all 3 resignations if put in writing. The matter was eventually settled after a *very frank* discussion and all differences should have been cleared away.

There was also some frustration with bureaucracy and waste:

28 Nov 1942: Boro Treasurer said . . . that subsistence allowance must be paid to Wardens and sheets returned within 7 days, and that all pay shall be put in separate envelopes for each Warden (what about paper shortage and waste of time?).

Other surnames mentioned in the logbook associated with E-sector are Bodfish, Bedford, Baggott, Gill and Worrall.

Pam Melloy's father was an ARP warden based in the Sutton Arms. 'Mum was not too pleased when he came home one night and climbed into bed still wearing army boots. Maybe he'd had a bit too much to drink that night!'

The ARP relied on teenagers (or younger children) to relay messages. John Russell (junior) was a messenger for C-sector in Coventry Street delivering messages to other sectors in the town. Eric Mole, at 15, was another. He had a bike to travel between ARP posts or to people's houses. His local HQ was on Kidderminster station yard in a coal merchant's office covered with sandbags. There were two wardens, a telephonist and himself. 'I had an armband but no uniform. I had no lights on my bike – it was blackout.'

APPENDIX A
THE CARE AND MAINTENANCE OF THE STIRRUP PUMP

1. All pumps should be tried out with water at least once a fortnight, to ensure that they are in working order and ready for immediate use; it may be advisable to test more frequently in frosty weather. (A stirrup pump can be used for many domestic jobs, such as washing down cars, syringing windows, watering gardens, laying dust, etc.) Regular use of the pump has two advantages: it gives people practice in its use, making them thoroughly familiar with the best method of handling it, and will also bring to light any faults in the pump itself.

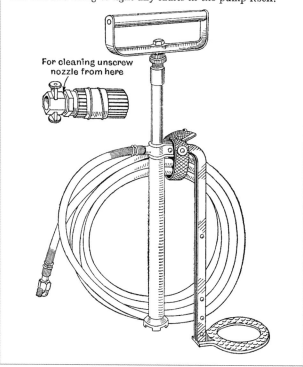

For cleaning unscrew nozzle from here

Extract from *The Fire Guards Handbook*: the stirrup pump with dual jet and spray nozzle. (*John Russell*)

When a Bomb falls in the open....

Hold a Sandmat in front of your face....

Extract from *The Fire Guards Handbook:* tackling an incendiary bomb in the street. *(John Russell)*

Place it on the Bomb....

and get away quickly.

Alf Mole's dad was an ARP warden in Lorne Street. 'They used lads of 16 and 17 as messengers; I was too young but occasionally ran errands for them. I could get from place to place quickly because I knew all the alleyways.'

❖ ❖ ❖

When the initial rumblings of war with Germany emerged there was general fear of gas attacks on the civilian population. Preparations for this eventuality were in hand well before the outset of war and gas masks were issued nationwide. By the beginning of 1937 masks were being produced at a rate of 50,000 per week and 38 million had been issued by the time of the Munich Crisis in 1938.

In March 1940 Kidderminster parents with children under 4 were advised to attend Pike Mills to collect appropriate gas masks. A pram was recommended for transport of the baby respirator which enveloped the whole of the infant's upper body. 'Mickey Mouse' masks were available for toddlers, and medium- and full-sized masks for older children and adults.

BOROUGH OF KIDDERMINSTER

AIR RAID PRECAUTIONS

The distribution of

BABIES' ANTI-GAS PROTECTIVE HELMETS
AND CHILDREN'S RESPIRATORS

will take place at

PIKE MILLS, GREEN STREET

During the week

18th to 23rd MARCH, 1940, INCLUSIVE

BETWEEN THE HOURS OF 9 A.M. AND 6 P.M. EACH DAY

Parents of children up to the age of 4 years who have not received a helmet or respirator, are requested to attend at Pike Mills, Green Street, in alphabetical order as set out hereunder:-

All those whose surnames

commence with the letter

A. or B .	on	MONDAY, 18TH MARCH.
C. D. E. or F.	on	TUESDAY, 19TH MARCH.
G. H. I. Or J.	on	WEDNESDAY, 20TH MARCH.
K. L. M. N. or O.	on	THURSDAY, 21ST MARCH.
P. Q. R. or S.	on	FRIDAY, 22ND MARCH.
T. U. V. W. X. Y. or Z.	on	SATURDAY, 23RD MARCH.

The Baby's Helmet is somewhat bulky and parents of children under two years of age are advised to bring a baby carriage to convey the Helmet home.

Children from two to four years of age should be brought to the Depot to be fitted.

Demonstration on the use of the equipment will be given.

G. T Cheshire & Sons Ltd., Kidderminster

Advice to parents on how to collect children's gas masks from Pike Mills, Kidderminster.
(*Godfrey Jones*)

Sheila Kirk was issued with a gas mask in autumn 1939. 'Being below the age of 5, mine was bright red with Mickey Mouse eyes. It smelt horrible with the chemical filter in the base. My brother was 6 and had an ordinary black one, much to his fury. The masks must have caused a lot of problems for teachers, not least because we could make all manner of vile noises by sucking and blowing through the side of our cheeks.'

Sheila also describes a different type of baby mask: 'Babies and infants too small to wear a face mask were fitted with a hideous metal Moses cradle, like a giant soap dish. There was a bed in the base and a chemical filter in the lid. The idea was to put the baby inside and close the lid, clipping it down. When my baby brother arrived, the soap dish cradle soon followed. Mother burst into tears and flatly refused to incarcerate the baby.'

Children's gas masks needed to be fitted properly, recollects Roy Bayliss: 'Mr J.G. Randall came to our house one night to fit gas masks for my brother and me. We were in a tin bath in front of the fire but my parents couldn't refuse and he was invited in. We sat in the bath whilst he fiddled with the gas masks.'

Everyone was supposed to carry their gas mask with them at all times. It came with a cardboard box and string to go round the neck. June Dowe recalls people personalising their equipment: 'I had a leatherette case: you felt a bit special if you had something posh for your gas mask.' Monica Hill recalls the constant reminder 'Got your gas mask?' but can't imagine how parents were supposed to go everywhere with the huge baby mask.

A gas mask designed to protect babies from gas attack. All the upper body was enclosed. (*John Russell*)

A full-size gas mask. (*John Russell*)

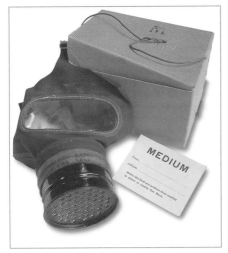

A medium-size gas mask, for older children or small adults. (*John Russell*)

A Mickey Mouse gas mask for toddlers. (*Worcester City Museum & Art Gallery*)

Regular checking of schoolchildren's gas masks became the responsibility of the ARP service; and reference to the E-sector ARP logbook shows that this was clearly taken seriously:

10 Nov 1942: Schools are to be attended for the inspection of gas masks every month, corresponding day each month if possible.

14 Nov 1942: As instructed by Head Warden Russell, visited St George's Infant School to arrange to inspect defective gas masks tomorrow morning, and also to arrange for a full inspection of masks the 3rd Wednesday next month. Also visited Lea St School to arrange for inspection of faulty masks tomorrow and arrange for a full inspection the 2nd Tuesday next month.

15 Dec 1942, 14.00hrs: Head Warden, Wardens Baggott and Bodfish at St Mary's Boys' School inspecting Gas Masks. 12 defective.

But sometimes help was to hand:

21 Oct 1942: Head Warden, Warden Hodges and Warden Baggott went to inspect Gas Masks at St George's Mixed School, but the Headmaster Longmore said there was no need to visit the school, he had inspected them.

That the inspections were necessary is shown by Mr Longmore finding 35 out of 225 masks to be defective.

Children's gas masks were sometimes tested by the gas van which came round to schools periodically. Mike Compton was at school in Abberley:

Our headmaster was insistent on gas masks being right and carried out the 'Mansion Polish' test: the lid from a tin of polish was put over the end of your mask and you breathed in. If it didn't fall off the mask was airtight. He was also keen on the gas van. Children would be put in the back of the van with their gas masks on and tear gas pumped in. On occasions they got you to remove your gas mask so you could feel the gas and see how effective they were. We didn't like that and once when the gas van came I was the only infant at school; all the others knew it was coming. So I went in on my own with the headmaster.

Roger Baulk recalls the gas van coming to St George's Infant School, Kidderminster.

One of the more important functions of ARP wardens was dealing with incidents and to prepare for this there were various training exercises. John

Warden's Report Form, filled in after a simulated incident. *(John Russell)*

Russell (junior) recalls that a galvanised building in Brinton Park, called the 'bomb hut', was used for training wardens. Furniture placed inside to resemble a room was set alight and a team sent in to deal with the fire. After the fire was extinguished the side of the hut was lowered to let the smoke disperse before reassembly for the next group. This happened on some Sunday mornings. There was also a shed for gas testing. Wardens walked through gas generated from a capsule. As they passed through they would ease the gas mask away from their face so they could smell the gas and recognise it should they meet it later.

Exercises to simulate damage and injury after a bomb attack were undertaken at intervals and a Warden's Report Form was completed after one such practice. And, of course, there were real incidents to deal with, notably the few air raids that occurred in the town. Graham Edginton remembers his ARP warden father, Stan, being involved in extinguishing the (oil) incendiary bomb which fell in the entrance to The Croft, Sutton Park Road.

The police and fire service were also called upon for such emergencies, as well as their normal duties. Bryan Tolley tells us that his father was in the

Auxiliary Fire Service and attended a large fire (not due to enemy action) at the Carpet Trades factory in Mill Street.

As soon as the bombing raids began on the Midlands there was concern about the effect of incendiary bombs and the possibility of damaging conflagration. Two notices in the *Kidderminster Shuttle* illustrate this. On 31 August 1940 advice is given about prevention of fire caused by incendiary bombs and the implementation of a scheme to provide fire watchers for large buildings. On 28 December 1940 there is a request to householders in Stourport to have available stirrup pumps, buckets, sand and water.

The Kidderminster Corporation Minutes dated 6 January 1941 show that the local authority was making good progress with plans for protecting the

INCENDIARY BOMBS

Early Action will Prevent Serious Fires

During recent Midland air raids fires have been caused by incendiary bombs dropped on roofs and not discovered in time. To meet this danger a movement has been organised in towns and other places in the Midland Region for watchmen to keep a look-out and, when enemy aircraft are not overhead to go on to the roof and into the lofts where practicable or to some look-out post and look for incendiary bombs or roof fires.

A large number of buildings such as office premises may be locked up and uninhabited at night, and it will be necessary in future to have a night watchman on duty who acts after an air raid develops for the purpose of patrolling the interior of the building and, in particular, examining roof structures of large office buildings and the timbers immediately below the roof access to these places being arranged for this purpose. In some cases such watchmen may no doubt be able to cover a number of adjoining buildings.

Sand has proved an effective extinguishing agent against incendiary bombs, and managers of buildings should see that sand is available in a convenient place.

In large buildings, offices and warehouses a fire party with stirrup pumps and buckets of water should be on duty.

Knowledge of the building is essential to enable rapid action to be taken. and fires can be dealt with before they become dangerous.

Notice in the *Kidderminster Shuttle*, 31 August 1940, giving advice on how to deal with incendiary bombs. (*Kidderminster Shuttle*)

Notice in the *Kidderminster Shuttle*, 28 December 1940, requesting householders to provide themselves with equipment for dealing with incendiary bombs.
(Kidderminster Shuttle)

> **Stourport-on-Severn Urban District**
>
> **AIR RAID PRECAUTIONS**
>
> In the event of aerial attack on this district, this may be preceded by the dropping of showers of incendiary bombs which mght cause a large number of small fires beyond the capacity of our Fire Fighting Services to deal with promptly.
>
> Air Raid Wardens will shortly be making a house-to-house call to ask householders to have available buckets of water and sand, and to induce them to provide themselves with Stirrup Pumps or to combine with others for this purpose and so be in a position to co-operate with other Services to deal effectively with such a contingency.
>
> A record will be kept of where these appliances are available.
>
> A limited supply of Stirrup Pumps may be purchased from the Council at £1 each, and further information can be obtained from your nearest Air Raid Warden.
>
> J. R. DANCE.
> Chief Warden.
>
> December 26th, 1940.   615

town, urging everybody to play their part and chivvying a few sluggish businesses to undertake their responsibilities swiftly:

> The Joint Committee gave consideration to precautions to be taken in dealing with incendiary bombs. . . . It was reported that the following steps have already been taken:
>
> 1. Demonstrations in the control of incendiary bombs have been given to the public and further demonstrations arranged.
> 2. Practically the whole of firms who come within the provisions of the Fire Watchers Order (making it obligatory to appoint 'fire watchers') have appointed the necessary persons to carry out these duties. The owners and occupiers of a few business premises at present within the scope of the Order have the matter in hand, and are being pressed to complete their arrangements as quickly as possible.
> 3. Many Supplementary Fire Parties under the direction of the Chief Officer of the Fire Brigade have been formed.

4. The Warden's Service has organised a number of fire groups from amongst householders and a free issue of 100 stirrup pumps has been made for this purpose. In addition the Wardens have been made responsible for selling a further 100 pumps to persons forming groups.

5. The Corporation have sold over 200 stirrup pumps to private householders and these persons are being asked to allow the pumps to be used by fire groups, and to display cards on their property intimating that a pump is available in case of need.

6. Owners and occupiers of business premises in the town centre have been interviewed and several are forming fire parties.

7. A quantity of sand has been dumped at many points in the town.

Many more Supplementary Fire Parties and household fire groups are required and the Committee stress the urgent need for Members of the public to join these groups to assist in watching for and dealing with incendiary bombs.

Church fireguard group outside St Mary and All Saints Parish Church, Kidderminster. From left, standing: Margaret Turner, A.J. Nixon, Revd J.M. Underwood, Winifred Denley, Revd E.J.G. Forster, N. Carter, Chief Local Officer W.J. Blencowe NFS, and A. Turner (leader); front: Muriel Frew, Jose Colbourne, Audrey Lindfield and Victor Cabe. *(Kidderminster Library)*

The price charged for a stirrup pump with a hose was £1, or without a hose 15s 6d.

In an industrial town with the factories mostly turned over to munitions and armament production, prevention of fire was of vital importance. The fire watchers of our town were there for that purpose. Bill Bury's father was a volunteer fire watcher at Tomkinsons factory. 'He was supplied with a steel helmet and given rudimentary firefighting training. He came home for breakfast and went back and did a full day's work!' Tax Inspector Vic Summers was in the Home Guard and also did fire spotting duties at the Income Tax office in Vicar Street.

Alf Mole felt sorry for the fire watchers he saw on the rooftops: 'In the mornings I would see the men still on the roofs. Those poor people were stuck up there all night. From the top of Castle Road, I watched them climbing back up the ladders in the evening.'

The medieval parish church of St Mary and All Saints was protected by its own fire guards.

Large static water tanks were placed at strategic positions around the town for firefighting purposes. These were found in many areas, including St George's Park, St George's Junior School, the Greatfield/Stretton road area and the car park of the Sutton Arms. The water tanks must have been attractive to adventurous children because on 25 March 1942 the headmistress of St George's Infant School recorded: 'A member of the NFS [National Fire Service] talked to the children about the danger of playing with static water tanks.' Graham Edginton recalls: 'It was not possible for a vehicle to pass from Spring Grove Road to Godson Crescent because a large round concrete water tank blocked the entrance to the Crescent. This static tank had a second use: US soldiers nearing full recovery from their wounds were frequent customers at the Sutton Arms. At least two were thrown into the tanks after arguments, or to sober up.'

One revealing discussion at a local education committee meeting about the installation of a water tank at Harry Cheshire School was reported in the *Kidderminster Shuttle* on 22 February 1941, just three months before the school was badly damaged in an air raid. The borough surveyor had obviously misunderstood a query put to him because he wrote to the committee with a costing for providing drinking water for the school.

Chairman: 'When they considered an extra supply of water, the question of drinking water did not enter their heads. They were thinking of what might happen if the mains were cut and they had no water for air-raid purposes. We want water to deal with incendiary bombs.'

Alderman Meredith: 'Has not sand proved the best thing for incendiary bombs?'

Alderman Cheshire: 'Not in every case, has it?'

Alderman Meredith: 'It is hopeless to use water unless there is a tremendous supply.'

Councillor Andrews: 'What is the use of stirrup pumps then?'

Alderman Meredith: 'To put out the fires round the bomb.'

Councillor Lacy: 'A tank would be useful at the school at any time.'

Alderman Meredith: 'A 5,000-gallon tank would be of little use for firefighting.'

Chairman: 'It would be of some use.'

Councillor Lacy: 'I think you should have two tanks, one on each side of the school.'

Alderman Meredith said they had any amount of mobile dams which the fire service could take to provide a supply in the event of the water being cut off. He did not think they should go to the expense of putting a 5,000-gallon tank at the school as a reserve.

Common sense prevailed in the end and they decided to seek advice from the chief fire officer.

Once the bombs started to drop, the first line of defence against injury to civilians and service personnel was the air-raid shelter. These came in many shapes, sizes and types of construction: purpose-built brick or concrete buildings, underground tunnels, cellars, outside corrugated steel Anderson shelters sunk into the ground, and indoor table-like Morrison shelters which resembled a large rabbit cage. Many householders adopted ad hoc solutions: areas under stairs, reinforced tables and even grand pianos (*see* Chapter 3, 'Under Fire').

We have knowledge of two air-raid shelters that still stand in Kidderminster (January 2006). The first is at the top of Barnsley's Hill, on the right-hand side of Chester Road North going towards Broadwaters, just past the junction with Hurcott Road. A second shelter was built in the grounds of Land Oak House against the perimeter wall adjacent to the footpath on Birmingham Road.

The authorities had already, by the start of the war, begun preparations to provide air-raid shelters. In September 1939 there were public shelters in Kidderminster that could accommodate 1,140 people, supplemented by trenches for 7,000. Matters developed apace and by 2 November 1939 shelters were available for 1,751 people (*see* Table 2, page 28).

A surviving air-raid shelter (as on 25 January 2006) in Chester Road North. It appears to be remaining from a terrace of shelters built down the steep slope. *(Bob Millward)*

An air-raid shelter still in the grounds of Land Oak House, Chester Road North, 25 January 2006. *(Bob Millward)*

Table 2. *The number of people provided for in public air-raid shelters in Kidderminster by 2 November 1939*

Location	Capacity
Cellars under retail market	200
Mill Street escarpment	170
Town hall basement	100
Rear of Messrs Wise radio premises	35
Rear of Messrs Wrensons' shop, Worcester Street	90
Basement of public library	175
Basement, 18 Church Street	52
25 and 26 Worcester Street	40
Basement of Mr Shingler's shop, Horsefair	180
Builder's yard, 101 Comberton Hill	214
Cross Brewery, Worcester Cross	160
Parkers Arms, Park Lane	35
Basement of Mrs Llewellyn's shop, High Street	300

Further schemes were being considered to provide shelter for approximately 10 per cent of the population in accordance with Home Office requirements. The Birmingham Control Centre expressed satisfaction with these arrangements.

In addition to public arrangements, provision was made for domestic protection: refuge rooms, adapted cellars and communal shelters. By 5 September 1939 many houses in the inner, heavily populated streets of the town had been provided with reasonable safeguards. Progress was rapid and by 3 December 1940 bolt-holes had been provided for an estimated 10,513 people. Table 3 (page 29) shows the progress made by March 1941; there was probably little development thereafter.

Deep tunnel shelters were considered as a means of protecting the local population, but dismissed (3 December 1940) on the grounds of cost (£300,000 to £400,000 for the whole population) and the difficulties of obtaining equipment, labour and materials. The committee was not prepared to consider tunnel schemes that would only provide protection for a minority.

Most air-raid shelters, if not useful as sheds or for some similar purpose, were demolished after the war. Kidderminster Corporation, after much negotiation, accepted on 30 December 1946 a tender by Messrs Albion Construction Ltd, of London, to demolish public air-raid shelters in the Borough at a cost of £2,983 11s 3d .

The dash to the shelter was always preceded by the strident wailing of the air-raid warning siren portending imminent danger. Eventually, the 'All clear' signalled safety – for the time being.

The first use of the air-raid shelter in St George's Infant School was on 30 September 1940.

The school logbook records: 'An air-aid warning siren was heard at 2.30 p.m. this afternoon. The children went to the shelter, in the playground, until the All-clear sounded about 25 minutes afterwards.'

There were other incidents: '3 Oct: An air-raid warning siren was heard at 10.50 this morning and the All-clear went at 11.30. The children spent the time in the shelter. Another warning was heard at 2.50 in the afternoon and the time, until the All-clear at 3.40, was spent in the shelter.'

All told, between 30 September 1940 and 26 March 1941, 20 air-raid alerts were recorded in the school logbook. From then on there were no more siren warnings and the school settled closer to normality. They did, however, continue with practices: '14 April 1943: At a signal from the Head Teacher the children practised Siren Drill; and went to the air-raid shelter in the playground.'

Melvyn Thompson's family had various means of keeping safe: 'I recall a large steel sheet, with four angle-iron corners, erected in our front room. The intention was to get underneath when the bombing started; but for my brother and I it was a great table-tennis table except when the ball hit the bolt heads! The neighbours combined to build an air-raid shelter in our back garden;

Table 3. *Provision of domestic air-raid protection in Kidderminster by 20 March 1941*

Area	Refuge rooms adapted	Cellars adapted	Communal shelters	People accommodated
Wood Street area	18	495	17	1,693
Bromsgrove Street area	51	564	27	2,649
Clensmore area	107	353	41	2,291
Foley Park Area	316	–	–	1,291
Proud Cross area	61	263	14	1,323
Sutton Common area	58	302	15	1,754
Hoobrook area	7	8	8	145
Aggborough	6	43	15	347
Gheluvelt Avenue	20	338	26	1,638
Lea Street area	11	316	7	1,626
Stourport Road	15	74	–	466
Miscellaneous	1	1	5	64
Totals	671	2,757	175	15,287

corrugated sheeting was provided for the roof and canvas to make bunk beds for the children. Like the table-tennis table, the shelter was never needed but it made a great den.'

Ruth Rudd recalls her dad erecting a large wooden framed bed in the cellar of their Leswell Lane house for use during air raids. There were no communal shelters in Leswell Lane (perhaps because a majority of houses had cellars). They shared their cellar with the Donovan family, who didn't have one in their 1930s-style house at the top of the lane; they brought their own chairs. The emergency exit was through the standard 'coal chute'. Next door had extra protection built over their exit in the form of an external cover: two brick walls about 3ft high with a thick concrete top.

A 1940 Christmas party in a Swan Street air-raid shelter. Anti-clockwise, from bottom left: Pam Batchelor's grandfather, Nancy Norgrove, Joan Holland, Mrs Batchelor, Hubert Norgrove, Sam Holland, Annie Holland, Fred Hardiman, Mr Lucas, Pam Batchelor, Eva Hardiman, Ciss Hardiman and June Hardiman. Back right: Mrs Hardiman (left) and Kate Norgrove. Front right, beside table: Roy Holland and Janet Holland. *(June Dowe)*

Bryan Tolley's family had a table made from half-inch iron plate with mesh hanging round the side. 'In daytime it was used as a normal breakfast table but at night you could sleep underneath it.' (A Morrison shelter?)

Jessie Maskell lived with her family in Stourbridge Road. They, and neighbours, used to go to the cellars of the New Inn when an air raid was imminent. She doesn't recall a communal shelter in the vicinity.

There were two brick shelters in Aggborough Crescent, but Peggy Guest and recalls a dug-out built in her garden by workers from her grandfather's firm, George Brown & Sons. There were seats and rugs on the floor, and room for seven people including neighbours.

In terms of air raids, it was certainly the 'shelter' that generated the greatest feeling of togetherness. It was a meeting place where people shared their fears and could bolster each other's spirits through communal companionship. Shelters were also used, on occasion, for get-togethers, as seen in a 1940 photograph of a Christmas party. This shelter was in the basement of one of the shops in High Street (possibly Llewellyn's) but the entrance was approached from Swan Street. June Dowe (née Hardiman) is the young 'nurse' at the front right of the picture.

Rivalry arose in some communities. Sheila Kirk tells us:

At the top of Bruce Road was a brick-built flat-roofed shelter. Neighbourhood drill occasionally led to inter-family strife when people who arrived first bagged more favourable pitches. And a definite social hierarchy existed. I twigged this through hearing the women natter. We piled in with blankets and snacks, and sang a few token patriotic choruses; but in a real air raid we never used the shelters. They were always kept locked! I guess someone had a key. Most people relied on using the room under their stairs; supposed to be the strongest place in the house – in our case the pantry. When a siren sounded my mother wrapped us in blankets and parked us in there. We loved it, and would devour the stock of jam tarts stored there. Mother spent her time standing at the gate watching for my father out on fire watch with the ARP.

Monica Hill has better communal memories: 'Next door to our house in Larches Road lived a builder called George Williams. Immediately the war began, his men began digging out for a big air-raid shelter nearby. There were about five local families that used this shelter when the planes started coming over.'

A mark of the comradeship found in this Larches Road shelter was the anonymous poem found in the shelter and later published in the *Kidderminster Shuttle*:

OBSERVATION

It's ten o'clock – the hooter's blown;
We all run helter-skelter,
With Thermos flasks and coats and rugs,
Down to our garden shelter.

With shielded lights we wend our way
To meet familiar faces;
We do our best to get there first
And pinch the 'comfy' places.

I don't mind air raids in the day,
I don't mind 'em at night –
But to have one when I want a bath
It don't seem blinking right.

And what a motley crowd we are –
The thinker and the talker –
Aunt Min sits tight throughout the night
Clutching her Johnny Walker.

One bloke felt quite tired, and went to sleep,
It was getting rather late,
But he quite forgot to shut his mouth
And lost his bottom plate.

Then someone said, 'There's a plane about,
I can hear the engine roaring.'
But they made a mistake, 'cos the aeroplane
Was Mrs Carter snoring.

Mrs W. thought she'd get some sleep,
So Mr W. said
'Don't talk in your sleep, my dear,
In case a Jerry is under the bed.'

It's four o'clock – the hooter's blown,
The All Clear's gone alright,
But I'll bet my bottom dollar
We'll be back tomorrow night.

3

UNDER FIRE

From the very first days of the war the nation lived in fear of attack by enemy bombers. The Luftwaffe was a large efficient air force which used blanket high-level bombing and targeted Stuka dive-bombers to overcome resistance as Germany drove through Europe to the Channel coast.

The British government was justified in being fearful of German air power: more than 60,000 civilians were killed by bombing raids on Britain between 1939 and 1945. (*The Blitz – Then and Now*, vol. 3, p. 6, 1990). Most of the bombing was concentrated on industrial areas such as Birmingham, Sheffield, Manchester and Nottingham and on the great sea ports of Liverpool, Bristol and Southampton as well as the nation's capital, London.

During the war 64,392 tons of bombs were dropped on Britain and Birmingham, with its heavy concentration of manufacturing, was particularly subject to many raids. At one time the raids on Birmingham were happening nightly and the bombers usually flew over Kidderminster on their way to Birmingham and back.

Peter Carter and his sister Monica Hill, who lived in Larches Road during the war, and Marjorie Rivers, from Shatterford, recall standing outside their houses witnessing the flashing lights and thunderous sounds of explosions over Birmingham and Coventry, and the searchlights and red skies as those cities burned. This was apparently a common experience in Kidderminster. Jessie Maskell remembers: 'The night the fish market was bombed in Birmingham we could hear the din as we were working in the "bomb shop" of Tomkinsons, filling mortar bombs with phosphorus. We panicked a bit, but the foreman wouldn't let us go to the shelter.'

Cyril Moore, aged 98, says: 'You should have heard the noise of them coming over night after night. They'd drop their bombs on Birmingham and then fly back again. The Severn was the guideline for them. They would cross the Channel to Bristol and fly up the river to Stourport and then turn right and head for Birmingham.'

Alf Mole used to watch from the back window of his three-storey house in Lorne Street:

Over the tops of surrounding houses I could see fires burning when Birmingham and Coventry were bombed. After a while we children became a bit blasé when sirens went; we had become used to the noise of the planes going over and not attacking us – so we carried on playing. This was a bit dangerous because shrapnel was always falling from the sky. We collected shrapnel in tins! When the bombers were going over at night, no matter how dark it was, you could make them out. And when they got towards Birmingham the glow from the fires outlined them. Our firemen went to help. We would watch the firemen come back in quite a state, often asleep on their ladders.

Locals considered it possible to tell whether aircraft were due to raid Liverpool or Birmingham by which side of the River Severn they were flying (Welsh side for Liverpool). Flight diagrams (Ramsey, *The Blitz – Then and Now*, vol. 2, p. 336, 1987) support this argument.

It is doubtless true to say that the area round Kidderminster was never deliberately targeted by the Luftwaffe, but nevertheless there were occasions when the towns of Kidderminster and Stourport experienced the effects of bombing.

The first bombs to drop on Kidderminster fell near Hoobrook in the early hours of Thursday 29 August 1940. On that night the main attack had been against industry in the Midlands, but Liverpool and London had also been targeted.

The incident was reported in the *Kidderminster Shuttle* on 31 August 1940 although, for security purposes, newspaper reports at the time did not identify, directly, locations of enemy action.

MIDLAND TOWN'S FIRST AIR RAID DAMAGE

During the air raids experienced by parts of the Midlands on **Wednesday** night and in the early hours of **Thursday** morning high explosive **bombs** were dropped in several towns. One **Midland town** had its first air raid damage of the war, when three **bombs dropped** on the outskirts of the town. Two fell in a beet field (one failing to explode), and the third among trees nearby, but no damage was done apart from the craters caused. Windows in the town were shaken by the explosions. No one was hurt.

This cutting, from the *Kidderminster Shuttle*, Saturday 31 August 1940, describes the first bombs to drop in the Kidderminster area at Hoobrook.
(Kidderminster Shuttle)

MESSAGE FROM LORD DUDLEY (Midland Region Commissioner for Civil Defence.

I am sending this message in a spirit of very deep gratification to those who have been involved in the air raids that have taken place in the Midlands. People's spirits seem to be at their highest during these days of trial, as if they had been left to meet the challenge. In my visits to scenes of raids and damaged districts I have been met either with a laugh, a joke, or some other example of our national habit of considering other people first.

Many reports have come in which have shown the public's willing and extremely valuable co-operation in the work of Civil Defence. I would, however, qualify this with a note of warning. Civilians must t expose themselves to personal risk out zeal to help the trained Forces; when this help is needed it will be asked for. Be ready, but take all possible precautions for your own safety and the safety of your household and house.

One striking feature of these raids is, that despite a certain amount of damaged property there has been comparatively little loss of life. This is not only due to A.R.P. precautions and shelters, but also to the good sense of the public in avoiding where possible assembling together in large numbers at times when raids are most likely to occur.

We can, and will, maintain this spirit of courage in the face of danger, and prudence in the face of personal risk. No action of the public can be of greater help than this to those engaged in Civil Defence work, and no better example could have been shown than has been done in these last few days. This spirit will defeat the enemy.

A cutting from the *Kidderminster Shuttle*, Saturday 31 August 1940, of a message of reassurance from Lord Dudley to 'Midlanders' after recent heavy bombing. (*Kidderminster Shuttle*)

Throughout the air raids over Britain the authorities made strenuous efforts not only to prepare the population for dealing with the effects of HE (High Explosive) bombs and incendiaries, but also to maintain morale by playing down deaths and the damage occurring to our infrastructure. Thus, Lord Dudley placed the message shown above in the *Kidderminster Shuttle*, Saturday 31 August 1940, in response to heavy air attacks on the Midlands on 29 August. It was, no doubt, copied to all Midland local newspapers.

Another two months elapsed before further attacks on Kidderminster were reported. On Sunday 3 November 1940 enemy action over the country had been confined to reconnaissance work; there were several instances of machine gunning and a few bombs were dropped. It was in the afternoon that many startled local inhabitants witnessed a lone German aircraft attack both Kidderminster and Stourport. Margaret Phelan recalls:

BOMBS ON TWO TOWNS

Lone Raider Drops from Clouds

Hundreds of people in a West Midland town had their first glimpse of a German 'plane on Sunday afternoon when a lone raider dropped from the clouds, flew over the town, and released two bombs which fell on either side of the road leading to a football ground.

One bomb exploded harmlessly in the grounds of a derelict house which has been unoccupied for some years and was falling into ruins — a process hastened by the blast from the bomb! Far more potentially dangerous was the bomb which dropped on tennis courts across the road. The courts formerly formed part of the grounds of a Vicarage, and the Vicarage

First section of a report in the *Kidderminster Shuttle*, Saturday 9 November 1940, describing the two bombs that dropped on the previous Sunday at the top of Hoo Road, Aggborough, and those falling in Stourport.
(*Kidderminster Shuttle*)

One Sunday afternoon early in the war we were having a cup of tea at my mother's. I was looking out of the front window onto Birmingham Road opposite the Convent when I heard a plane coming over, 'Brr Brr'. I said, 'That's a German.' My mother said very severely, 'Don't be silly, Margaret, it's Sunday afternoon!' But it *was* a German. As it came into sight we could see the black cross and swastikas and black smoke coming from the tail. As it went over the Convent long black sausage-like objects fell from it.

Les Lench also recalls the incident:

I would be about 14 or 15 years old at the time. I saw a bomber go over and said, 'That's a German plane' and my father said, 'Don't talk rubbish'. This was a Sunday afternoon – we were on our back door step. I said, 'Look it's dropping its bombs.' One landed in the Aggborough district and went into the cellar of the house of the owners of Steatite. They were Germans and had been interned for the duration of the war. The house was badly damaged and there was a big crater – I didn't get any shrapnel, though. One landed just across the road in Vicarage Crescent; it was the last house – next to where Johnny Rogers lived.'

Bryan Tolley was walking with his mother and brother when the bomber passed over. His mother said: 'Look at those two birds close to that plane.' But his brother who was in the Air Training Corps corrected her, 'They're not birds, they're bombs,' and identified the aircraft as a Heinkel bomber. Another informant thought the aircraft was Italian.

This was also probably the raid described by Cyril Moore: 'One afternoon we were in the garden and we looked up and saw this plane. He dropped a bomb by the works in Green Street. The factory had a glass roof and the lights were on – so that probably attracted it. He came out of the cloud and dropped the bomb between Hoo Road and Green Street and went back up into the clouds. It exploded but I didn't go to see it. It didn't do any damage.'

Pam Holloway was sitting in a deckchair in the garden of 6 George Street. 'They are dropping sausages from those aeroplanes,' she is reputed to have exclaimed. Her dad grabbed her and her sister and raced them down into the cellar. He then called their next-door neighbours who used to share the cellar with them.

The event is described graphically by Sheila Kirk:

We were in The New Church on Comberton Hill for Sunday worship, a sunny afternoon I think. My parents were in the choir stalls, Norman and I were in the nave seats, colouring away at our lesson sheet, when the warning siren blared out. The few men rushed off, grabbing their tin hats and gas masks. That was scary enough. The service went on. I remember standing at the end of the pew panicking a bit. Suddenly there came an almighty roar of a plane followed by a tremendous explosion. The building shook. (A crack later appeared down the wall above the door. The weakened building never really recovered.) Terrified, I raced up the aisle screaming, 'Mummy, Mummy'. She met me halfway. Normal service was suspended while the minister ran out in case he was needed. Some time later the men returned reporting that a bomb had landed on Hoo Road.

Stourport also suffered on this occasion. It was surprising that this was the only time the town was bombed as, like Kidderminster, it was heavily industrialised for its size – with a great emphasis on war work. However, the bombs which fell on this Sunday afternoon were not targeted and it was thought that they were dumped by an aircraft trying to escape pursuit by fighters. One fell in the station yard, one fell in Vernon Road near the Lickhill Road, one fell at the other end of Vernon Road, but most significant was the bomb which struck the school. The building suffered severe damage but, fortunately, as it was a weekend, no children were in school. The school was where Stourport library, medical centre and police station now stand.

A Stourport resident who was a boy of 9 or 10 at the time remembers the day well. 'It was about four o'clock and I was in Tan Lane and heard gunfire. I was scared and ran off home and I could hear the guns and the bombs. One bomb fell in Jimmy Cox's back garden and another in Mavis Sykes's garden. One fell on the Boys' School, which was closed for quite some time afterwards while some of it was being demolished.'

The *Shuttle* records both incidents in its issue of Saturday 9 November 1940. Although the locations were not identified, the details reported in this account largely corroborate our informants' recollections: 'Two bombs fell at Aggborough: one in Vicarage Crescent and the other in the grounds of a derelict building on the other side of the Hoo Road. Some glass was damaged in the side of the Grandstand of the (Harriers) football ground. In Stourport the greater proportion of the buildings of the Boys' School was demolished. Other bombs fell in gardens nearby to little effect. Machine gun firing was heard. There were no major casualties from this raid; just a few superficial injuries to occupants of houses in Vicarage Crescent close to the explosion.'

The next raid on Kidderminster occurred in the early hours of Thursday 12 December when incendiaries were dropped in the Marlpool Lane/Puxton area. We have no eye-witness accounts of this but the *Shuttle* reported on Saturday 14 December: 'During Wednesday night's heavy raid on the West Midlands a number of incendiaries fell in the suburb of one West Midland Town and one of them destroyed a fowl house and its feathered occupants. Some fell harmlessly in open country, and others were promptly dealt with by the civil defence service.'

This was the night when there was a major attack on Birmingham, the longest the city had then experienced. There were also widespread minor raids elsewhere, mainly on airfields and seaports.

The night of Thursday/Friday 13/14 December 1941 marked, perhaps, a major turning point in the air war. In previous months the RAF had been impotent against night raiders; the Luftwaffe roamed almost at will. But this night, with major attacks on Glasgow and Liverpool, nine enemy aircraft were destroyed, a success due to the development of Ground Controlled Interception (GCI).

There were widely scattered minor attacks elsewhere and Hurcott appears to have suffered one of these when 15 bombs were dropped in open countryside. Sheila Kirk and brother Norman Ryder recall:

A bomb dropped in the fields along Hurcott Lane, towards Stourbridge Road, about half a mile from our house. We were in our pantry during an

THURSDAY NIGHT'S RAID

Fifteen Craters in Open Country

A wood pigeon was the only casualty when a salvo of bombs fell on the northern boundary of a West Midland town on Thursday night. The high explosives fell on either side of a country lane, some in a field and some in a wood. Fifteen craters were counted. Small fires were started but quickly died out, except one, which may have been caused by an incendiary bomb. It was extinguished by a member of the A.F.S. Although the bombs fell in open country, they were comparatively near to a residential district, where people were aroused by violent explosions coming in rapid succession, and the impact was widely felt. The concussion shattered a number of windows, burst several door locks, and disturbed plaster on ceilings, but no one was hurt.

A description in the *Kidderminster Shuttle* of the fifteen bombs dropped near Hurcott on the night of 13 March 1941. *(Kidderminster Shuttle)*

alert; Mother, as usual, was pacing about outside waiting for Dad to appear. I was asleep but woken by a terrific roar of a low plane, followed by an enormous CRUMP. The house shook and windows rattled. Norman and I were frozen on the spot; I remember seeing my brother with a jam tart halfway to his mouth, paralysed. Then I started screaming: "Hitler's got our Dad." We found out later that the bomb had landed in a field, not touching any building. We found the huge crater (visible for years) guarded by a solitary soldier.

There were also bombs dropped near Baldwin's factory in Wilden. Mrs Hazel Fallon was 15 at the time and says: 'the concussion stemming from the explosion was felt in Kidderminster.' Probably these were not ordinary bombs. Les Lench says: 'I remember that land mines fell on Wilden. One at Hoo Brook and one at Wilden. These were parachuted down and I went over there for shrapnel and found the lamp off the parachute – but the police took it off me. I got a huge piece of shrapnel which was stuck into an oak tree.'

This was probably the incident described in Tomkinson and Hall's book, *Kidderminster Since 1800*: 'Tuesday night, 22 April 1941: 2 Parachute mines landed near Platt's wharf.' Platt's wharf served the canal close to Wilden, between Kidderminster and Stourport.

Probably the most dramatic incident was when the western side of Kidderminster suffered considerable damage on the night of Friday/Saturday 16/17 May. The trail from this raid appears to have followed a line through Sutton Park Road, St John's Avenue, the Harry Cheshire School (now Baxter School) and Habberley Valley.

Many houses in and near Sutton Park Road and St John's Avenue were affected and the relatively new Harry Cheshire school suffered extensive damage; only the head's office and the staffroom were left unscathed. Habberley Valley was set alight by incendiary bombs. There is a plaque in the valley commemorating the violation of this popular beauty spot, and Eva

BOMBS ON SCHOOLS AND HOUSES

Raid on West Midlands

Bombs which fell on a West Midland town in a recent raid did considerable damage to a school and residential property, but only a few people were hurt. A new senior school, recently completed at a cost approaching £100,000, suffered worst. The wings of the building were demolished by two direct hits, and class rooms rendered untenable by the effects of blast and broken glass. Other bombs fell harmlessly in the environs of the school.

A former Mayor of the town was rendered homeless by an incendiary which penetrated the roof of his house. The resulting fire gutted the upper portion, despite the efforts of himself and his son, supplemented by auxiliary firemen. Outside the residence of another former Mayor, an oil bomb was successfully dealt with by a street fire party with sand. In the same area four people sheltering under a grand piano had a fortunate escape when the back of their house was wrecked by a high explosive bomb. A bungalow received a direct hit, but its two occupants were extricated from the debris. A fire-watcher on duty nearby was struck by flying shrapnel, and was taken to hospital for treatment, as were the occupants of the bungalow. All three were detained. Two high explosive bombs fell in open ground, one dropping in soft earth on the gable side of a house without doing material damage. Tiles were dislodged and windows broken by blast in many houses in the locality.

Fire-watchers and civil defence personnel did splendid work.

SCHOOL CLOSED FOR THREE WEEKS

A small portion of the long report in the *Kidderminster Shuttle* outlining the air raid on 17 May 1941 that did so much damage in Sutton Park Road, St John's Avenue, the Harry Cheshire School, Habberley Valley and nearby areas. *(Kidderminster Shuttle)*

Landon gives a vivid description in the book *Kidderminster Foreign – Portraits of Trimpley and Habberley*, edited by Nigel Gilbert.

The incendiary bombs causing the conflagration in Habberley Valley were probably of the type shown here. These are from a collection used by John Russell (senior) for ARP training and are typical German B1E 1kg magnesium incendiary devices about 34cm long. The bomb on the right has been identified by Martin Garnett, of the Imperial War Museum, as made by Rheinmetall-Borsig AG, Sommerda. The main features of this type of device are shown in the diagram overleaf.

Graham Dowe: 'I remember the Germans dropping the bombs on Sutton Park Road. They say the bomber was being chased by a night fighter and jettisoned its bombs trying to escape. The bomb made a huge crater and our house was showered with rubble. The entire roof came down on the property of my music teacher Mr Williams who lived next door but one. They would have been killed if he and his wife hadn't been using a Bechstein grand piano as an air-raid shelter.'

Two typical German 1kg 13.5-inch magnesium incendiary bombs. *(John Russell)*

Pam Melloy remembers very well these bombs falling. She was living, aged just 5, with her parents at 54 Sutton Park Road situated on the upper corner with Rifle Range Road. The house, which she believes was originally built for the gardener of The Croft, was later to become part of the Kemp Hospice; it was demolished in 2005. Pam informs us:

On the night concerned my mother was looking out of an open bedroom window when the bomb dropped. She received a face full of dirt. Fortunately, the bathroom window at the opposite side of the house was also open which probably saved our house from serious damage. There was an evacuee staying with us – a lad from Birmingham. He was so used to bombs that he simply rolled over, so that his camp bed was on top of him for protection, and went back to sleep. Our house had two storeys and when Dad went downstairs he couldn't open the door to the lounge; so much dirt had built up against it. We must have got out through the front door. The rest of the night was spent with relatives who were neighbours up the hill – Nell and Bernard Hughes.

We came home for a breakfast of black pudding. Someone must have given that to us as we didn't normally eat it. A large Kidderminster Golf Club trophy, which my father had won earlier, received a dent in the side as

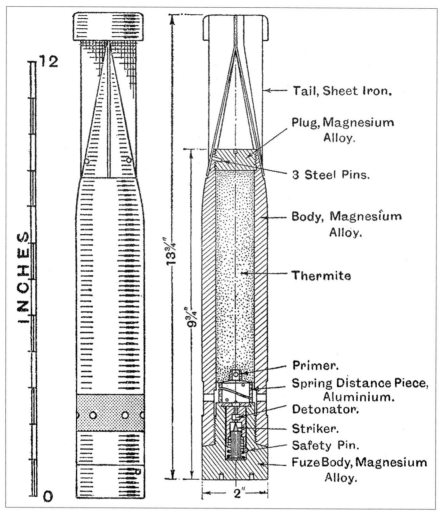

Diagrammatic drawing illustrating the mechanism of a 13.5-inch magnesium incendiary bomb. *(John Russell)*

a result of the blast. I imagine subsequent winners each year for the rest of the war may have had to display a slightly dented trophy.

Many sightseers came by that weekend and couldn't believe that all our windows were undamaged. They *weren't* undamaged! It just looked that way because they had been totally blown out. Some were found on a side fence hanging by the safety netting glued to them.

My mother's uncle Harry Whale was a builder and he was able to replace the windows for us quite quickly. Nearby a pair of semi-detached houses occupied by the Busby and Williams families were hit. Also a large incendiary bomb dropped in the gateway of The Croft.

Photographs showing just how close the crater was to 54 Sutton Park Road after a high explosive bomb fell in the nearby field on 17 May 1941. *(Pam Melloy)*

The girl seen at the edge of the bomb crater is Pam Melloy (née Jones) aged 5 years, now living in Australia. *(Pam Melloy)*

This was certainly the oil-bomb dealt with by the street fire party referred to in the *Shuttle* report. Graham Edginton's father Stan was an ARP warden involved in extinguishing that bomb. Graham thinks that The Croft was at that time in use by the Army: 'I know there were several ATS girls in residence as they provided mince pies when I was delivering Christmas post.'

Graham describes his memories of this raid: 'Our house was the first house in the stretch between Spring Grove Road and Rifle Range Lane (opposite side to Sutton Arms). There was spare land between Spring Grove Road and No. 45 at the time. A bomb fell in the night behind the houses in the stretch to Rifle Range Lane. I vividly recall soil settled on the roofs and our family thought there was a fire upstairs. There was little structural damage. The house gutters were filled with soil and later in the year plants could be seen growing. The crater was only a short distance beyond the extent of the house gardens. I was down the crater as soon as it was light. I was aged 13, at Hartlebury Grammar School, and was anxious to obtain pieces of shrapnel to exhibit.'

Cyril Moore recalls that 'As well as the bombs in Sutton Park Road several fell on the Harry Cheshire School – it put all the lights out. Then another bomb dropped about 100 yards further on – I can't quite remember whether it exploded or if it was a dud. A bomb also fell in Spring Grove Crescent, where I lived at the time. There were three houses and we were showered with bricks and stones; it broke the tiles on our roof. I was married then and our niece was living with us. I just grabbed her and rushed into the cellar. I was working at Wolverhampton and, as I went to work the following morning, I saw the crater. I picked up a piece of shrapnel and kept it for a long time – but eventually lost it.'

Jack Young was 14 at the time. During the raid his mother rounded up the family to go to the shelter, 'but I wouldn't go until I had put on my slippers'.

Bryan Tolley saw demolition lorries tipping damaged exercise books and rubbish from the Harry Cheshire School on a field off Greatfield Road.

Both William Bradley and Keith Lloyd (Keith now lives in Adelaide, Australia) refer to Mrs Lewis's bungalow in Greatfield Road that was badly damaged by an unexploded bomb. According to Keith, 'Mrs Lewis was asleep at the time and all four walls opened outwards like a pack of cards. It was considered a miracle that she was unhurt – just covered in plaster from the ceiling. I believe Mrs Lewis was taken in by a family in Heathfield Crescent.' Keith Lloyd was living in Leabank Avenue and remembers the night well. 'I spent part of it under the dining room table! A blast blew in all our windows and brought down the ceilings. The sirens had warned us there was a plane in the area.'

Beryl Millichap (née McCormick) lived next door to this bungalow. 'I was about 4 when a bomb dropped on next door. We were in the pantry and when we came out our windows were blown in and the bungalow was flattened. The only damage to me was a fly paper stuck to my head.'

Sheila Kirk also has recollections of this incident. 'We were sitting in our pantry on the other side of town (scoffing raspberry buns) but we knew someone had "bought it". My aunt lived in Greatfield Road and what intrigued us children was her description of the lady in the bungalow which was hit by the bomb. Apparently she was wearing metal curlers in her hair and the force of the impact pressed the curlers into her head. We all wanted to go and inspect this phenomenon but of course we were not allowed. Spoilsports! I believe that apart from that no occupants were really hurt although the house was badly damaged.'

We only have two pieces of information concerning the damage inflicted on St John's Avenue. Firstly, that published in *Kidderminster Since 1800* by Tomkinson and Hall: '147 houses in St John's Avenue damaged'. It is surprising that no one has come forward with personal recollections. Secondly, a report in the *Kidderminster Shuttle* dated 10 November 1945, dealing with the induction of the new Mayor Alderman A.E. Meredith: 'During the war his house, Crantock, St John's Avenue, was bombed by German aircraft and destroyed by fire.'

This bombing incident, which seems to be the last one of the war to affect Kidderminster, coincided with a major attack targeted on Birmingham by 111 aircraft dropping 160 tons of HE and 2,076 incendiaries. However, through error, the main weight of the raid had actually fallen on Nuneaton.

Other areas around Kidderminster experienced bombing incidents. Mike Compton's father, Bill, was walking home through the back lanes from Stourport to Abberley past an ack-ack (anti-aircraft) station manned by regular soldiers under canvas. When passing the camp he heard a yell, 'Get down!' and a bomb fell nearby and exploded. It was an isolated bomb and was regarded as being a 'stray'.

Marjorie Rivers living in Shatterford recalls: 'Every evening, when it was dark you could hear the bombers following the River Severn down at Arley. And they dropped a bomb on the field at the back of us. But it was only a little bomb. It did no damage, only scattered earth around.'

A report of an unexploded bomb falling near Lea Castle Hospital is given in Journal Number Eleven of the Wolverley and Cookley Historical Society (2001). The bomb could not be located at the time and was only discovered in 1980!

The scavenging of shrapnel seems to have been quite a hobby during the Second World War but most collections have been lost. Pam Melloy's mother, Mrs Jones, to this day still has the piece of shrapnel that they took with them to Australia after the war.

Killed by Shell.—Miss Hannah Maria Moore (aged 73), occupier of the two front rooms at 89a, Lea Street, Kidderminster, whose funeral took place at Kidderminster on Monday, lost her life as the result of an air raid. She had retired to bed as usual, and during the night, while a heavy anti-aircraft barrage was in progress, the cap of a shrapnel shell penetrated the slate roof, and struck her as she lay in bed. It appears that she must have died instantly from shock. The tragic discovery was made next morning by a neighbour who went to take down the black-out in the old lady's bedroom. Deceased, who formerly lived at an almshouse in Rackfields. Kidderminster, moved to Lea Street only two months ago. In her younger days she was a nursemaid in the household of the late Mr. Frank Stone.

The report in the *Kidderminster Shuttle* about the only person who died in Kidderminster during air raids. Sadly, this was a result of 'friendly fire' when a shell from anti-aircraft fire penetrated the roof as she lay in bed. (*Kidderminster Shuttle*)

Throughout all the air raids on Kidderminster and Stourport there were no serious casualties arising directly from bombing. One man who had been sheltering in the Boys' School doorway at Stourport had a near miss. He decided that the rain had eased off sufficiently for him to leave and was about 25 yards away when the bomb hit the school.

In terms of the bomb damage that was inflicted on many industrial towns in the West Midlands Kidderminster was really very lucky! Sadly, that luck did not extend to Miss Hannah Moore, who was an unfortunate casualty from what would now be termed 'friendly fire'.

Hannah Moore died when shrapnel from an anti-aircraft barrage penetrated the roof of her accommodation in Lea Street. Her funeral was on 16 December 1940, so it would seem that her death probably coincided with the bombing that occurred near Puxton on 12 December.

But the German invasion from the air was not all about bombing towns, cities, docks and airfields. Often they were seeking information about defence systems, gun emplacements, troop locations, dispersed armament factories and so forth. One such intruder passed over Bewdley at 11.30 a.m. on 4 September 1940 taking aerial photographs of such clarity that they are now being used to determine the state of orchards at that time. This was at the height of the Battle of Britain and the German High Command was attempting to establish conditions for invasion (Operation Sea-Lion) and required comprehensive and detailed intelligence. Fortunately this local intelligence was not to prove of use to the potential invaders. On the same day about 650 planes attacked southern airfields in the morning and factories in the afternoon. Widespread attacks continued that night on Bristol, Bath, Gloucester, Manchester and Liverpool and various other places in the north-east, east and west Midlands, west and south Wales and London and the Thames Estuary.

Aerial photograph taken near Bewdley by German reconnaissance on 4 September 1940 at 11.30 a.m. Wyre Hill is seen running top to bottom in the right of the photograph. *(A. & N. Turley/US National Archives)*

4
THE HOME GUARD

The Home Guard is often perceived to be as it was portrayed in the television comedy *Dad's Army*. In fact, it was taken very seriously by those in the organisation and those who envisaged the Home Guard as a vital part of the country's defence in the event of invasion.

The organisation, originally known as the Local Defence Volunteers (LDV), was formed after the Minister for War, Anthony Eden, broadcast shortly after 9 p.m. on 14 May 1940 a request for a civilian-based army. Such was the enthusiasm of the population that within twenty-four hours a quarter of a million men had volunteered and within six weeks one and a half million men had enlisted. Kidderminster was no exception and the *Shuttle* of 18 May 1940 reported: 'The police were immediately inundated with enquiries and the number enrolled soon ran into hundreds. The first man volunteered almost before Mr Eden's broadcast was finished and three others had "signed on the dotted line" before 10 o'clock that night. By Friday the Kidderminster Police Office advised that LDVs accepted numbered 350.'

By 25 May this number had grown to more than 600 and soon the *Shuttle* announced: 'Col W.H. Wiggin is the Commander of Worcestershire County sub-area, and Major W.A. Painter MC has been appointed Divisional Organiser LDV Corps for Kidderminster; his Headquarters for this purpose is to be the police station. The first patrol of ten men armed with rifles and ammunition did duty on the outskirts of the borough on Sunday evening and other patrols have been on duty every day since.'

It is not clear from where the rifles were obtained so early in the war; they may have been privately owned. Certainly there were no uniforms – not even the LDV armlets promised by the government. However, the WVS (Women's Voluntary Service), Women's Hospital Supplies Group and pupils of Kidderminster High School made forty temporary armlets with material supplied by Mrs M.A. Anton JP, a school governor.

There were sixteen sections in the Kidderminster Home Guard, each of ten trained ex-servicemen, plus an auxiliary squad of thirty-five to guard vital service points such as power substations and the electricity depot. The section leaders were O.W. Davis, C.W.E. Hopkins, H.T. Viney, G.H. Mantle, E. Gwillam, J.G. Harvey, A.A. Knight, R. Loynes, H.J. Lamb, E.A.K. Forrest, R.A. Ovens, R. Sykes, W.H.X. Smith, J.D. Simes, G.C. Stevens and L.A. Dudley. They must have obtained appropriate uniforms fairly quickly as by 10 August 1940 the *Shuttle* was able to report: 'An increasingly familiar sight is the uniform of the LDV indicating the increase in enrolments locally. Members of the Kidderminster Battalion are engaged every evening patrolling their observation posts and guarding vulnerable points. Many are veterans of the Great War and some even of the South African War and their ribbons make a show of colour on the otherwise drab uniform. The smartness in appearance and active service experience of these veterans is of the greatest assistance to the younger members, who lack nothing in enthusiasm for their new job.'

The Home Guard was open to all men aged between 16 and 65 and was organised on formal military lines. Among its numbers were those too old or too young for active service in the regular forces, and those engaged in essential war work who were excused from military service. Many had full-time jobs during the day and served with the Home Guard at night and at weekends. The personnel list of the 8th Worcestershire Battalion of the Home Guard Headquarters Company Machine Gun Section shows this clearly (see below).

Listed Home Guard personnel of HQ Coy Machine Gun Section.
(*John Russell*)

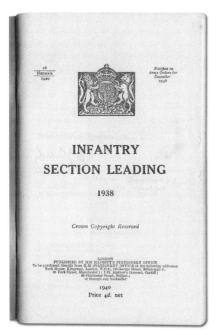

26
Manuals
1920

Notified in
Army Orders for
December
1938

INFANTRY
SECTION LEADING

1938

Crown Copyright Reserved

LONDON
PUBLISHED BY HIS MAJESTY'S STATIONERY OFFICE
To be purchased directly from H.M. STATIONERY OFFICE at the following addresses
York House, Kingsway, London, W.C.2 ; 120 George Street, Edinburgh 2 ;
26 York Street, Manchester 1 ; 1 St. Andrew's Crescent, Cardiff ;
80 Chichester Street, Belfast ;
or through any bookseller

1940
Price 4d. net

1938 Army Instruction Booklet
republished for the Home Guard.
(John Russell)

Lt Lewis and Private Rigby both worked in Birmingham with daytime Edgbaston telephone numbers, but appear to have lived in Kidderminster. Privates Matthews and Clarke were based at home – possibly being retired.

The local Home Guard adopted standard military formation: companies and platoons. In addition to the Kidderminster Companies many other volunteers had headquarters in outlying villages. These were widely separated from each other, so cohesive training was not really practicable. Platoons relied on their own resources and, although training facilities and lectures were available at the Drill Hall in Stourport, the platoons were unable to make much use of them. Nevertheless, in the official history of the Worcestershire Home Guard it says: 'In these circumstances great credit is due to Platoon Commanders and NCOs that such a high quality of training was achieved.'

Home Guard soldiers were taught musketry, signalling, bombing and machine-gun operation. They learned military tactics and had field exercises. They also had some non-standard lessons, such as 'Use

PLATE IV.—FORMATIONS.

A section advancing in arrowhead formation.

Extract from the 1938 Army Instruction Booklet. *(John Russell)*

of the Country' from Mr R. Millet, who was said to be 'adept in the art of teaching recruits to emulate the example of the invisible man'.

There were efforts by the government to assist with training. Military manuals were made available – the 1938 booklet on leading an infantry section was swiftly republished for the Home Guard in 1940.

A typical detail shows a section advancing in arrowhead formation (see opposite).

A further pamphlet on *Small Arms Training*, issued in 1937, was reprinted for the Home Guard in 1941 and formed part of a series for providing personnel with military skills.

Kidderminster had a substantial military presence: the Royal Army Pay Corps, the Auxiliary Territorial Service and the nearby US hospitals and camps. It was not unusual for the Home Guard to do training with personnel from these establishments; but the Pay Corps had little experience of battle conditions and it is doubtful

Small Arms training pamphlet reproduced for the Home Guard. *(Kidderminster Library)*

how much value came from this. However, it exposed the Home Guard to other military units and helped them appreciate that they were part of the official military arm of the country.

Sgt Cyril Harber (seated, centre) and his platoon. *(S. Healey)*

There were exercises with the Free French based at Ribbesford. Mrs Healey of Wribbenhall advises that her father, Sergeant Cyril Harber, led a platoon which patrolled the Rifle Range and Lickhill. He told her about mock battles with the French and how, on one occasion, a 'combatant' was killed – despite the use of dummy bullets.

People who couldn't join the forces were often keen to sign up with the Home Guard. Leonard Burrows was 14 when he volunteered with his pal Stan Cooper.

'There was no trouble in joining,' he says; surprisingly 'our roadblock was at the top of Bewdley Hill'. Reg Carter heard Anthony Eden's plea on the wireless and next morning went to the police station. His daughter and son recall:

> They hadn't got a clue what he was talking about, but they took his name and address and had to find out what was going on. Initially they only had an armband with LDV on it. That was their uniform; then they became the Home Guard and Dad was made Quartermaster. He had an office over Bert Onslow's fish shop in Trinity Lane, and the stores were behind Vicar Street through an archway between the Futurist cinema and Woolworths.

Reg also did duty at a station on Hoo Farm:

> They had a cowshed or a barn. When he returned from his first night on duty he said: 'It was perishing cold, I'll take that old oil heater from the shed.' When he came back the next day we asked if it was any better? 'Better!' he said, 'Better! As soon as it got warm there were millions of bluebottles.'
>
> Later, we would laugh until we cried at *Dad's Army*. Even Dad laughed. He said, 'It's not funny because it's made up, it's funny because it's true!'
>
> Don't ask me how he did it but Dad got food for those involved in one of the weekend manoeuvres. In our hall there were big trays of tomatoes, great slabs of Madeira cake; stuff that we kids hadn't seen anything the like of. We stood and drooled until we were given a couple of tomatoes.

Reg Carter in Home Guard uniform. *(Monica Hill)*

Reg made an error of judgement on one occasion when he brought thunder-flashes home. His son Peter put a match to one and finished up on top of a 6ft fence covered in blood.

Les Lench was also anxious to be involved:

I was too young for the army so I joined the Home Guard. I was in No. 2 Platoon of the Worcesters and was one of the youngest. Most of the others were beyond military age. Our HQ was the Futurist cinema and I was the platoon driver. We used any vehicle we could get. We guarded Victoria Bridge at Bewdley on Tuesdays, on Wednesdays the BBC transmitters at Droitwich and on Saturdays the petrol dump in Stourport. In between I did fire watching – you could be called out at any time for that. I got a Home Guard uniform straight away when I joined in 1942; it was one way of getting decent clothing. I enjoyed the Home Guard but I still wanted to get into the military, so when old enough I engineered the sack from my reserved occupation in the laundry and within three weeks was in the Warwickshire Regiment. I joined up wearing my Home Guard uniform and was the best recruit – probably as a result of my Home Guard training.

One example of Home Guard exercises was recalled by Roy Bayliss of Areley Kings. 'The Home Guard was strong round here and was regularly seen on patrol. One snowy winter's afternoon we were having Sunday lunch and my mother, looking out of the window, said: "What's that on the lawn? Who are those men?" White-clad figures were crawling across the lawn towards the neighbours' garden. It was the local Home Guard covered in white sheets wriggling on their stomachs doing winter manoeuvres.'

Melvyn Thompson's father had been a Marine in the First World War and wanted to do his bit defending the area in which he lived – so he joined the Home Guard:

Most of our neighbours were also in the Home Guard and seemed to be ranked according to profession. Would you believe it, the Major was the local bank manager! His sergeant was Harold Evers, organist and choirmaster of St George's Church. My dad was a private and proud of it. I think their platoon headquarters was based at the golf club; it was funny to see them cycling up the road in rank order on sunny evenings to defend the golf links. In later years my dad told me they had more trouble with courting couples than with the Germans! One of the perks of being in the Home Guard was the free issue of heavy boots and a uniform – both ideal for digging the garden.

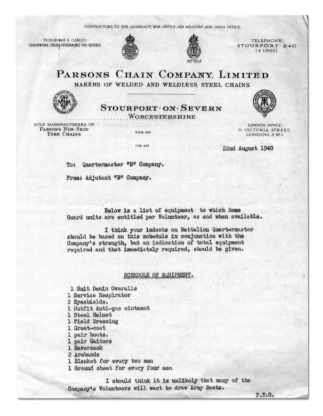

CONTRACTORS TO THE ADMIRALTY, WAR OFFICE, AIR MINISTRY AND INDIA OFFICE

TELEGRAMS & CABLES:
CHAINWORK, TELEX STOURPORT-ON-SEVERN

TELEPHONE:
STOURPORT 240
(4 LINES)

PARSONS CHAIN COMPANY, LIMITED
MAKERS OF WELDED AND WELDLESS STEEL CHAINS

STOURPORT-ON-SEVERN
WORCESTERSHIRE

SOLE MANUFACTURERS OF
PARSONS NON-SKID
TYRE CHAINS

YOUR REF

LONDON OFFICE:
11 VICTORIA STREET,
LONDON, S.W.1.

OUR REF.

22nd August 1940

To: Quartermaster "B" Company.

From: Adjutant "B" Company.

Below is a list of equipment to which Home
Guard units are entitled per Volunteer, as and when available.

I think your indents on Battalion Quartermaster
should be based on this schedule in conjunction with the
Company's strength, but an indication of total equipment
required and that immediately required, should be given.

SCHEDULE OF EQUIPMENT.

1 Suit Denim Overalls
1 Service Respirator
2 Eyeshields.
1 Outfit Anti-gas ointment
1 Steel Helmet
1 Field Dressing
1 Great-coat
1 pair boots.
1 pair Gaiters
1 Haversack
2 Armbands
1 Blanket for every two men
1 Ground sheet for every four men

I should think it is unlikely that many of the
Company's Volunteers will want to draw Army Boots.

P.T.O.

List of equipment to be issued to
all Home Guard personnel.
(Kidderminster Library)

Some commanders were reluctant to issue boots. The Adjutant of 'B' Company, when giving a schedule of kit entitlement for each volunteer, added in a letter: 'I should think it unlikely that many of the Company's Volunteers will want to draw Army Boots.'

June Dowe remembers some Home Guard activities: 'They would form road obstructions using concrete blocks. If the enemy landed they were to pull these across the road. On one occasion my mother went to see my aunt who lived in Wilden Lane – but when she came away there was a roadblock in place and the bus couldn't get through. She had to walk all the way back to the centre of Kidderminster.'

Although the Home Guard manned checkpoints regularly they never saw serious action. Yet there was one occasion when they really did think that they were about to combat an invasion. The event caused great consternation at the time and became known as the Battle of Bewdley. Sightings of what were claimed to be enemy parachutists had been reported near Bewdley and it was felt necessary for the Home Guard to take appropriate defensive action.

Below is the record of the Battle of Bewdley found in the local Home Guard history compiled from the official reports by Lt-Col. P.W. Robinson, the then Company Commander, and Captain H. Goodwin MC of the Bewdley Platoon:

The alarm was first given to the Bewdley Police by two men at about 16.00 hours on Sunday 30 June 1940. They passed the information on to the Officer commanding Bewdley Platoon. He felt that in view of the reliable character given to the two men by the police he had no option but to give the alarm by ringing the church bells; although neither he nor his officers had actually seen any sign of parachutes. Subsequent questioning of the two witnesses and others failed to shake their conviction, but other reports received since, state that a considerable quantity of hay was picked up by air currents and was probably in the air as two planes passed. There were eight witnesses who stated that they saw something falling from the two machines in question and, so far as it is possible to ascertain, all these witnesses were ordinary rational people.

By 17.00 hours Captain Goodwin had sufficient men to throw out a screen to keep Ribbesford Wood and its approaches under observation, and also to man the necessary road barricades. At 17.30 the Commanding Officer had been contacted and on his instructions the Stourport bells were rung: by 17.50 a sufficient force had paraded to man all barriers in that town.

At 19.00 a bren-gun carrier arrived at Bewdley from Norton barracks to be followed by two Platoons at 21.30 and 22.00 hours. These Platoons with fixed bayonets, but unloaded rifles, proceeded to search the wood advancing in single file along the paths. Failing to find anyone they returned to Barracks, the first Platoon arriving at 23.00, the second at 00.30 consequent on a second alarm reported by a civilian motorist at 23.00. He stated that he had heard a crackling of wood in Liveridge Coppice at about 17.00, thus causing a further search to be made.

At 01.35 a further message was received from the Police that an armoured car containing two enemy dressed as English officers was to be stopped at all costs, which entailed further manning of the barricades and posting of sentries. It was not until 04.00 that the final all clear was given.

Civilians thronged every point of military activity throughout the 'action': roads and bridges were so crowded that troop movements and road checks were impossible. Stourport High Street and Load Street in Bewdley were solid with people and matters were made worse by the fact that Motor Coach Trips were due to return in both places.

In Abberley the first information was received by 'C' Company at 17.20 hours from the Police Superintendent: by 17.30 HQ had been manned and the message passed to outlying sections. At 17.35 a report was received that

Rock bells had been rung. By 18.30 sufficient men had reported to form two fighting units and one watching section, whilst from the outlying villages reports had come in that road blocks were manned. At 02.20 hours the message reference the armoured car, later changed to a camouflaged car, was received and passed on to section leaders. Finally, at 05.30 hours the stand down was given. At the time there were only five .303 rifles available but no man throughout the platoon paraded without a lethal weapon of some sort: .22 rifles and shot guns were pressed into service.

All this sounds very militarily efficient but Bill Compton, who participated in the action, had rather different recollections. His son has graphic memories of Bill's account of his experiences that night:

I was aged 3 when the war started. My main recollection is of the Battle of Bewdley, which took place on a Sunday evening in June 1940. My family went to Evensong at Abberley Church and we were met at the lychgate by the Vicar the Revd J. Grant Richardson. There was to be no service that night because parachutists had been seen landing in a field north of Bewdley. He instructed Dad to change into uniform and report to the Manor Arms without delay. We went home and my mother took me to stay with her sister whilst Dad went off to fight.

He was given a .303 rifle and at 8 p.m. sent to the top of Abberley Hill. By 10 p.m. they realised he hadn't been issued with ammunition and so someone was sent with a few bullets. It was a cloudy night and dark under the trees. At about midnight he heard some rustling in the bushes. Dad wasn't a person to mess about so he shouted 'Halt!' – but with no result. The rustling continued and got closer so he shouted again, and once more got no response. He put a bullet in the breach of his rifle and aimed it at the area from which the noise was coming. But just as he was about to pull the trigger the moon came out from behind a cloud and he could see that it was Howard Limerick's donkey! Relieved, he let the donkey go on its way. (Howard was something of a recluse who lived in a shack in the woods).

Soon afterwards the order came to stand down. But nobody informed Dad. They had no radios then and it wasn't until they were going off duty that somebody said: 'Hey, Bill Compton's not here.' So a volunteer went up the hill to relieve him.

At my auntie's we eventually heard that the Home Guard were being stood down and that there was no invasion. We were very relieved as we had been told of the atrocities that the Germans would do to us if we were invaded. It turned out that it was not parachutes seen, but hay blown into the air by a freak wind.

Leonard Burrows was at home in Park Lane on the Sunday of the Battle of Bewdley:

> Bert Evans, a barber in Wood Street and Sergeant in charge of No. 1 Section, No. 6 Platoon of 'B' Company, came to the door and said: 'Len, get your uniform on and your rifle.' We drove in Bert's car to the Futurist Yard in Vicar Street where Sergeant Major Dudley gave me a clip of five rounds of .303 ammunition and told me to make them all count. We made our way nervously to Bewdley where we found people running all over the place, and a man on the bridge was having medical attention. We manned our post until late into Sunday night.

Bill Compton was a member of No. 9 Platoon, based at Abberley. The magnificent clock tower was their main observation post because it gave an unrivalled field of view. He told his son: 'It was manned by six men and an officer. The regular army manned the tower during the day and the Home Guard at night; with two men on shift at all times. I worked 12 hours a day at Parsons Chain Company in Stourport and when I'd had my tea went off to the tower to go on duty. The view from the tower was such that you could see bombing activity over Coventry and Birmingham, especially the searchlights.'

The description of joint action with the regular army is interesting and demonstrates that the role of the Home Guard was important. Naturally, various theatres of war were given priority for equipment and supplies, and for a while the Home Guard was equipped with only the most basic materials. Early on, war uniforms and weapons were in short supply and troops would drill in their everyday clothes, Home Guard armbands and broomsticks for rifles. Even the armbands were often home-made, using stencils and whatever material could be found. Some members were keen to arm themselves. Leonard Burrows worked at Bradley and Turton and made himself a dagger and a .22 hand pistol. 'I was reported to the manager by the blacksmith's striker, who was a special constable. I've still got the dagger, though.'

Eventually, when ammunition was issued to the Home Guard, the government was anxious to ensure none of it was wasted and issued posters to all units which urged that in the event of action there should be 'Blood on every bullet'.

Gradually the Home Guard became more professional but there were still moments of farce worthy of the BBC's Private Pike. Leonard Burrows recalls:

> During hand grenade practice one recruit threw the grenade straight up and it came down into the dug-out. Lieutenant Brockway picked it up and threw

it away – just in time. That was the action of a very brave man. Another time on manoeuvres on Hartlebury Common we found a dead rabbit – we cooked it for dinner next day.

One early morning on duty I saw a figure and challenged: 'Halt! Who goes there?' It was our Sergeant with a sack of millet on his back. That wasn't as bad as the night at the sugar beet factory when Private Dollar Morris turned out the guard for a suspected intruder. It turned out to be a horse – we had some fun over that.

One Sunday morning we stopped a truck loaded with potatoes. Sergeant Evans found too many bags on board and told the driver that he would have to report it. He gave us two bags, was let off, and went on his way.

The Home Guard formed an important part of life in Kidderminster during the war. Not only was it a reassuring presence but a strong social side developed and many dances and events were organised by individual units

Kidderminster Home Guard Rifle Club, winners of the Western Command Trophy 1946. Mr Tolley is third from the right, flanked by Mr Howells (supporting the cup holder) and Alec Charles. *(Bryan Tolley)*

The last March Past of the Home Guard in
Kidderminster, Sunday 3 December 1944.
(Kidderminster Library)

In the years when our Country
was in mortal danger

JOSEPH ALFRED COLWELL

who served 31 May 1940 to 31 December 1944
gave generously of his time and
powers to make himself ready
for her defence by force of arms
and with his life if need be.

THE HOME GUARD

Certificate of Service from King George VI.
(Kidderminster Library)

throughout the war. After the war much of the comradeship carried on. For instance, the Home Guard Rifle Club continued to meet and shoot competitively for many years.

Bryan Tolley still has the medals won by his father with the Rifle Club and the team won the Western Command Challenge Trophy in 1946. The club trained using sandstone banks at the back of the Harriers' ground and also indoors at Pike Mills.

The Home Guard in Kidderminster was finally stood down at the end of 1944. On that day the 6th Battalion assembled in Green Street and marched through the town to the Grammar School playing fields for a formal ceremony.

A grateful nation recognised the work of the men who so selflessly volunteered for home defence and a certificate from the King was presented to all who participated.

5

THE MILITARY PRESENCE

Kidderminster was possibly as far from theatres of war as it was possible to get in England but at times during 1939–45 it must have resembled a garrison town with many servicemen passing through or billeted in the area.

It was its inland location that was responsible for the first movement of military personnel to the area. The Royal Army Pay Corps, based on the south coast, was quickly moved to a less hazardous area after early German air raids.

Pay Corps Clerk Betty Sutton was 20 when she transferred to Kidderminster from Folkestone in 1940:

We were allocated to various pre-selected families. Their houses had passed inspection; others had been rejected for billeting as being sub-standard – too small or no bathroom or indoor toilet. We found everything in Kidderminster quite different. At first, I was billeted with Mrs Greenwich at Larches Cottage, Stourport Road, which has now been pulled down.

Eventually we settled in and, in addition to using lodgings, we took over a few houses around the Shrubbery. One was a doctor's house, and we had a centre in the Shrubbery with our own cooks and mess hall. We handed our ration books over to the cook; we had exactly the same rations as civilians. At least twenty girls from the Pay Corps used the Shrubbery and we were completely self-sufficient apart from laundry. We weren't paid much – standard military pay was 2s per day for the male soldiers and we were paid two-thirds of that.

Our base was Pike Mills which was converted into Pay Corps offices, and we were joined there by Auxiliary Territorial Service personnel. We had a NAAFI (Navy, Army and Air Force Institute) which provided drinks, meals and cigarettes in the garage. There were other offices on the upper floor of Tower Buildings and in the shops either side. We also took over St Mary's Church Hall.

We became involved in the social life of Kidderminster and formed the RAPCATS, an entertainment group. We were very well accepted by the local people and tried to join in with local activities. I remember helping with potato picking and harvesting sugar beet. We got half-a-crown for a full day's work.

We stayed at Pike Mills until 1945, when the Pay Corps office was closed. At that time we were beginning to get demobbed and, as the US 52nd General Hospital at Wolverley had also closed, the remaining members of the Pay Corps moved there.

Joan Phipps was also a member of the Pay Corps and came to Kidderminster at the same time as Mrs Sutton.

I arrived by train and marched in full kit to Pike Mills and then to Lea Street where I spent two years billeted with a local couple. About 100 to 150 of us came to Kidderminster.

I was 21 at the time and, like other young ladies in the Corps, joined in the social life of the town enthusiastically. I particularly enjoyed the dances held in town and surrounding areas. We went cycling and swam in the local pool. Although we were away from home we were in no real danger, and many of us enjoyed our time here. We identified 99 public houses and I was quite proud to say that I managed to visit all of them.

We were very popular with the Americans from the camps at Wolverley and Burlish and they, of course, liked dancing with us. They kept their forage caps in their shoulder epaulettes when we were dancing and I would steal their cap badges. I eventually got enough to fill a leather belt.

We liked exploring the local countryside and on one occasion thought we saw a parachutist and we heard air-raid sirens. We raced back to our unit – but were told later that is was only hay blown up by strong wind.

Sheila Kirk has memories of army personnel billeted with her family in Baldwin Road:

The first were from the Pay Corps, based at Caunsall/Cookley. Later we had two soldiers, at one time three. Where on earth did we all fit? I, being the only girl, had the small bedroom to myself but my brother shared the soldiers' room. Originally one chap came, Stan Little. Next door was Bill Sharpe, but he did not get on with them, so my mother took him in. Sometimes his wife came for the weekend, but when she didn't he flirted with my auntie if she was home for the weekend! We thought that was hilarious, anyone fancying our auntie. One was from Bristol, the other from London. My dad could not stand them but my mum looked after them too well; they preferred her meals to the camp meals. One moved on and Alan Tate, from Newcastle, came. He was the favourite; considerate, polite and educated. We kept in touch for years.

Beryl Millichap's family had Americans billeted: John Olin (from Texas) and Hugh (from Detroit). They later sent a giant lollipop and a wooden lamb on wheels from America as presents.

The two United States Military camps in the area were hospitals built to cater for wounded US personnel. Once again it is interesting to see that the Kidderminster region was considered a safe area for this purpose. The camps were substantial and there was also a large number of permanent staff – doctors, nurses, guards, etc – as well as the many US servicemen arriving for treatment.

Of course, such a large influx of foreign troops made quite an impression on the area and many people have memories of that period. 'My sister stayed at home during the war to look after the family,' remembers one gentleman. 'She joined the Red Cross and visited the US Hospital at Wolverley to give therapy to wounded soldiers. They were taught to knit and to do other handiwork to keep them occupied. Some soldiers were wounded more than once and those severely wounded were classed as ZI (Zone Interior) which meant that they were sent home instead of back to fight.'

Soldiers capable of walking were allowed into town. 'They could come into Kidderminster,' said Maurice Fallon, 'but not into people's houses without a formal invitation. Casual visiting was not permitted. As a result they would spend a lot of time leaning against buildings; this was such a common occurrence that people said that the town would fall down if it wasn't propped up by American servicemen!

'You could always tell wounded soldiers from the others – they wore different coloured uniforms. British wounded had blue uniforms.'

US Personnel were allowed to visit the YMCA canteen opened in a former factory in Orchard Street for members of all armed forces. One helper there remembers: 'Soldiers, sailors and airmen on leave, or passing through, would call in and they could get sandwiches, tea and coffee. Gallons of coffee were prepared every day and it was always finished – largely thanks to the Americans.'

Janet Cowburn (née Holland) was a mascot for the Red Cross and was taken in uniform round factories and offices collecting but had to earn her money at the Wolverley Camp: 'The friendly Americans invited me to go to their camp; they wanted to make their contributions. They put pennies in my tin and I gave them a Red Cross flag from my cardboard tray to pin on their uniforms. Afterwards I performed acrobatic tricks for the patients on the hard floor of the camp hospital!'

June Dowe thinks that finding the YMCA may have been a problem for some Americans. 'One soldier was heard asking how he got to the "Yumka".

Janet Holland collecting funds for the Red Cross in 1943 at the gate of the American Wolverley Camp. *(Janet Cowburn)*

They had no such problem finding the refreshment room set up in the Church Street Baptist Church, where all US personnel could go for snacks and coffees. They called it the Doughnut Dugout.'

Jane Dowe recalls that the local churches welcomed the Americans, although they did have their own services on camp.

They often visited the Baptist Church and were made very welcome, not least because they were always very generous and left a good donation on the plate. On some occasions we would go to a service at the Wolverley camp. They always looked smart in their uniforms which were twice as good as the ones our soldiers wore. Sometimes a group of them would start singing and I remember quite clearly their barber-shop-style songs. They were quite friendly. On one occasion a friend and I daringly approached two US soldiers in town and said "Got any gum, chum?" – a well-known phrase in the war. They gave me some, but I was afraid to take it home. My mother would have killed me if she had known. So we didn't do that again.

Alf Mole was also lucky with the Americans: 'If you went past the Burlish camp and said, "Have you got any sweets?" you would usually get some. On one occasion we had a tin of beans thrown over the fence.'

Roy Bayliss has stories of American soldiers in the area.

Most days men and women soldiers would march up Stourport High Street. At the time I was helping at Stanley Barton's and we had a very pretty assistant called Pam and sometimes the soldiers would drop out of the ranks and buy cigarettes from her. They would bring gum and sometimes give some to me.

When I was still at school, and we heard that a train was coming to Stourport station with American wounded, we would go and watch. We saw stretchers brought out and some awful sights; I suppose it didn't register with us, as children. There were soldiers from the Front covered in blood when there hadn't been time to clean them up.

Slightly older, Les Lench actually assisted when casualties came to Burlish. 'When the military first brought the wounded it was by train; about 600 of them. There were insufficient ambulances so we pushed them up the hill from Burlish Crossing on their stretchers. This was just after the invasion of Europe. After that they came constantly to Burlish and to Wolverley through Kidderminster station. I used to go regularly to the military hospital and play cards with the patients. Most were white – I only ever met two black soldiers.'

Les had mixed reactions from American soldiers because of his three sisters and sister-in-law – all attractive.

Although I wasn't very old, sometimes my job was to chaperone the girls. At times our house would be full of Americans. They brought food and we would cook it. My sisters were very popular – in fact any young woman was popular. I remember one of my sisters was on the doorstep one night with a Mr John Bond from Pennsylvania – I was keeping watch through the bathroom window. As soon as I thought he was getting a bit frisky I shouted her in. Sometimes the American soldiers would snarl at me for this but at other times they would take me into Kidderminster and buy me Rum and Pep drinks to try and get round me.

In this area, the main contact between British and American soldiers was not military but social. The Pay Corps and the ATS decided that they would form a band and concert party and used to perform regularly at the US hospitals.

Fred Sutton of the Pay Corps recalls: 'We often did a four-man show at Wolverley Hospital – doing all five wards in one and a half hours. The piano was mounted on a rubber wheeled trolley. The patients really enjoyed it. I remember one man actually jitterbugging to our music although quite badly injured. The Commanding Officer wrote to us saying we had done more good in ten minutes than a lot of their medicines.'

Peter Carter as a Post Office Telephone trainee has a more racy recollection of the Burlish Camp. 'On one job there I found a thumping great barrel of beer in front of the altar in the chapel, and a box of "French letters" by the door. I was only about 16 at the time.'

Melvyn Thompson also enjoyed US generosity at a time of great change: 'One day there was a very long American convoy parked along Chester Road North and South. The soldiers were obviously taking a break and local housewives, including my mother, were asked to cook sausages for the troops – the deal being keep-one-give-one-back. When the convoy moved off we lads had a good stock of chewing gum – we had never seen chewing gum before!'

There were many similar instances. Margaret Phelan was working at the Co-op Dairy at Franche and used to cycle there from Birmingham Road. 'It must have been just before the D-Day landings; plenty of American convoys were going past. I had a wicker basket in front of my bike and by the time I got to the dairy it would be filled with chewing gum, cigarettes, chocolate and sweets; I was very popular when I arrived! I only had to wave back at the soldiers as they threw stuff in.'

This was probably the time of the build-up to the Normandy landings, when large numbers of troops and armaments were making their way to the south coast. Alf Mole was up early to do his paper round in late May 1944 and found military policemen directing columns of traffic on Chester Road. 'The convoy went on hour after hour and I had to dodge through it delivering the papers. Afterwards, I went to Yew Tree Road and saw train after train going south loaded with tanks, lorries and guns.'

Apparently, in the months preceding D-Day, large amounts of armaments had been stored in the local countryside. Bill Bury saw stocks of military vehicles hidden in orchards and Alf Mole recalls troops and armoured vehicles stored under netting off Axborough Lane and in Bisset Wood; British soldiers were looking after them.

Alf noted that 'When the convoys started those troops began moving out. It wasn't long after that before we saw ambulance trains bringing the wounded back from Normandy to Burlish and Wolverley.'

Sheila Kirk saw these same convoys just after they entered Kidderminster:

Normally, there was little traffic on the dual carriageway of Birmingham Road; an occasional car, or even less frequently a Midland Red bus. So it caused great excitement to find enormous convoys of American troops trundling along the road. The children's spy network would set up a cry, 'The Yanks are coming!' We would drop everything and run. There were trucks, tanks, motor cycles – and hundreds of golden, hunky chaps. They often stopped for a rest, sitting on their vehicles or the grass verges. They were very friendly and seemed to laugh a lot. 'Got any gum, chum?' was our cry.

But they had more than gum. We were given whatever they had – chocolate, sweets, biscuits, a tin of ham, pineapple once, cocoa, tea *in bags* (tasteless, we all agreed later), pencils, a comb for my mum. They lifted us up into the trucks and showed us pictures of their children and took photographs of us. I once sat on a tank, which terrified me: 'What if it suddenly went off with me on it?' This caused them great amusement.

The generosity of the American soldiers seemed quite universal; they were obviously making an effort and maybe it was something to do with the dangers they were about to face.

They said they would come back for us once they had chased off 'that old Hitler'. I really believed they would! Of course, I realise now that many of them never survived to come back. We felt perfectly safe; I suppose now the child protection unit would have something to say!

The American military authorities took their responsibilities as visitors very seriously and issued instructions and advice to their troops on how to behave in the UK. One example was the booklet *Instructions for American Servicemen in Britain, 1942.*

This covered advice on, for example, forgetting the War of Independence, British reserve, respect for our history and traditions, warm beer, cricket and the peculiarities of the English language. It was all very sensible and stressed that the two nations had different cultures, but were fighting a common cause.

The booklet concludes with some dos and don'ts:

INSTRUCTIONS
FOR
AMERICAN
SERVICEMEN
IN
BRITAIN
1942

A pocket book issued by the War Department, Washington DC, in 1942 providing advice on how US servicemen should behave in Britain. *(Bodleian Library)*

Be friendly – but don't intrude anywhere it seems you are not wanted.

You are higher paid than the British Tommy – don't rub it in.

Don't brag or bluster – 'swank', as the British say. If somebody looks in your direction and says 'He's chucking his weight about' you can be pretty sure you're off base. That's the time to pull in your ears.

If you are invited to eat with a family don't eat too much – otherwise you may eat up their weekly rations.

Don't make fun of British speech or accents. You sound just as funny to them – but they will be too polite to show it.

Avoid comment on British Government or politics.

Don't try to tell the British that America won the last war or make wise-cracks about the British defeats in this war.

NEVER criticize the King or Queen.

Don't criticize the beer, food or cigarettes. Remember they have been at war since 1939.

Use common sense on all occasions. By your conduct you have great power to bring about a better understanding between the two countries after the war is over.

You will find yourself among a kindly, quiet, hard-working people who have been living under a strain such as few people in the world have ever known. In your dealings with them let this be your slogan: 'It is always impolite to criticize your hosts; it is militarily stupid to criticise your allies.'

In general, the advice seems to have worked. According to June Dowe, 'There were hundreds of Americans here and I can't remember any drunkenness or that they were any trouble at all.'

However, Monica Hill recalls one unfortunate American who paid the penalty for becoming too familiar: 'There was one very nice serviceman from the Burlish. He was on the staff and visited us as often as he could; a very nice young man. He used to borrow my brother's civilian clothes – anything for a change. Unfortunately, he got caught by the American police. Somebody must have tipped them the wink because they hauled him off in disgrace. He was moved on and seen no more. That was a shame: he wasn't doing anything harmful.'

There is little evidence that the people of the area resented the large numbers of military personnel suddenly imposed upon them. Indeed, the diverse accents and cultures of the visitors added a colourful dimension to the austerity of those difficult days. The military presence, in all its forms, gave a tangible and often grim reminder of the realities of a war mercifully far removed from this comparatively sheltered part of Worcestershire.

6

AT WORK

In the early 1930s Britain was not prepared for war and it was not until war became imminent that urgent consideration was given to gearing up the country's capacity for producing goods and materials essential for an extended military engagement.

When war broke out the problem became acute as significant numbers of people engaged in conventional manufacturing were called up for military service. By 1940 3.5 million men were in the armed forces and it was necessary to create a new workforce to manufacture munitions and other essential items.

In January 1940 Winston Churchill called for 1 million women to become munitions workers and eventually females up to the age of 50 had to register for work. By June 1944 16 million people were involved in the production of war materials – and a further 1 million men and half a million women had become members of the Forces.

Manufacturing centres such as Kidderminster and Stourport saw huge changes. It was recognised, for example, that carpet making was not essential: production was first reduced and then terminated in November 1942. Carpet factories turned to making a variety of military goods. Maurice Fallon remembers:

There were a lot of factories converted to war work. BSA of Birmingham moved into two carpet factories in Kidderminster. One on Stourport Road was refitted to make munitions. Vickers Armstrong also had several factories in Kidderminster: No. 7 Factory was in Castle Road in the former Brintons carpet store, No. 6 factory at Carpet Trades in Mill Street and No. 9 in George Street.

No. 7 factory made oil-cooler inlets and fuel tanks for Spitfires and I got a job there as a sheet metal worker when I left school. I was an apprentice on a wage of £9 per week. The factory worked long hours from 8 a.m. to 7 p.m. and skilled men earned good money – £20 to £21 per week was normal. We were always busy on new tanks. Damaged units were sent to us for repair but the management quietly scrapped them and replaced them with new tanks. The workers understood it was a contribution to the war effort.

Some of these tanks were processed further at ICI (Wolverhampton), where Cyril Moore worked. 'I went on my bike to the station to catch the 7 a.m. train and got to Wolverhampton for 8 a.m. My job was coating aircraft fuel tanks to make them bullet proof. We used a form of rubber that would close up when hit by a bullet and so reduce leakage.'

People were directed into certain areas of manufacturing where there was a specific need. Maurice Fallon's father-in-law was a high quality carpenter. 'He spent the entire war making wooden ammunition boxes at a wage of £12 per week. He travelled daily from Kidderminster to Stourbridge by train, leaving home at 5.30 a.m. Lots of people travelled from Kidderminster to Birmingham – quite a few went to the Austin Motor Company, making patterns. The fare to Birmingham was about 10s 6d a week – if you didn't use all your ticket you could carry it over to the following week.'

Mrs Fallon's sister was a carpet designer at Perrins in Worcester Street. 'Most of their production went for export. On the day war was declared the company recognised that its market had disappeared and they closed down. She was directed to the food counter at Marks and Spencer as retailing food was regarded as an essential part of the food supply line. Another skilled lady designer from Perrins spent the war operating a lathe in a munitions factory.'

Pam Melloy's father had also been a carpet designer but during the war became a foreman in a Brintons munitions factory in Castle Road. 'My Grandpa Jones from Hagley also worked there as a welder. I still have a child's bucket and model Spitfire he made in his spare time.'

At the beginning of the war Brintons converted looms to make Army blankets and webbing until the regular manufacturers could cope with demand. Then, from 1940, the spinning shed was developed into a tool shop for making bullets,

cartridge cases and tools. Six skilled men were imported to train carpet workers and the unit developed to work twenty-four hours a day employing 400 people. According to Brintons' wartime records: 'These newly trained people produced equipment that only the most skilled engineering workers had done before the war.' As the war progressed the range and intricacy of armaments made by Brintons developed. At the end of 1940 they began manufacturing mountings for Oerlikon Admiralty guns but they were soon making whole gun assemblies.

Single 20mm Oerlikon deck-mounted Mk IIIA gun. (*Archive Collection of the Carpet Museum*)

On one occasion an emergency order, required for the invasion of North Africa, led to men working thirty-six hours without sleep.

The flexibility of the Brintons set-up meant that they could manufacture items quickly. After D-Day many small components were required. One device, the 'J-bolt', was needed urgently to make British and American components for Bailey bridges compatible; 15,000 were made and flown to France and Holland. Without these bolts, erecting Bailey bridges in northern France would have posed a much greater logistical problem that neither Montgomery nor Eisenhower needed.

Other equipment manufactured included roller conveyors, portable oil stoves, hand-operated petrol pumps, electricity generating sets and a device to clear mines from beaches using a powerful water jet. Perhaps the most interesting item they made, and indeed initiated, was the humble but useful 'jerrican'. Brintons had heard of an

'J-bolt' required to make American and British components of Bailey bridges compatible. Brintons supplied 15,000. *(Archive Collection of the Carpet Museum)*

Field Marshal Montgomery crossing the River Seine by Bailey bridge. *(Archive Collection of the Carpet Museum)*

efficient 4-gallon petrol container used by the Germans in North Africa and asked the Ministry of Supply for permission to make them. They collected a new workforce of more than 200 people: boys and girls under 18, non-directable married women, women over 41 and men over 65. These unskilled people were quickly trained. One ex-servant girl needed only one morning to become sufficiently proficient to join the assembly line.

Even surrounding villages were involved in this essential war work, possibly as an outpost of Brintons. According to Mick Compton, Abberley Village Hall was turned into a factory for making jerricans. 'They made thousands of them there. But my father walked to Parsons Chain, in Stourport, to make non-skid chains for military vehicles.'

Jerricans were filled, and refilled, at a specially built site at Chadwick Bank, near Stourport. 'Aged 14, I went to work at Chadwick filling jerricans,' remembers one Stourport resident. 'My job was to receive filled jerricans, add an identification tag and move them on for transportation. The fuel came to the site directly by pipeline.'

Norman Ryder's father had been a weaver at Brintons but was transferred to fitting and servicing bullet-producing machinery. 'Once, when working in a factory near Shenstone, he accidentally inhaled a ball bearing instead of blowing away metal dust. Worried, he cycled to the hospital and a doctor removed the ball bearing which had stuck at the base of his tongue. He cycled straight back to work at Shenstone. No work, no pay.'

Jerricans being edge-welded in a Brintons factory. *(Archive Collection of the Carpet Museum)*

Les Lench had several jobs in the war.

In September 1939 I left school early at 13 to start work. My brothers were in
the Forces and I was a breadwinner. I started at Victoria Carpets making
webbing for the army. I was the youngest there. Three of us from the same
school were interviewed and I got the job because I asked where I should hang
my coat! I stayed for 10 months until I heard that Naylor's were paying an extra
6*d* per week; so I went there earning 10*s* 6*d* a week in the yarn room. Then
Naylors changed to naval work – testing MTB [Motor Torpedo Boat] engines.
The creels were taken down and we cleared the weaving sheds, moving the 6ft
and 12ft looms to the wall, protecting them with hardboard. Concrete pads
were set onto the floor to support the engine test beds. I was too young for this
work and couldn't go back to Victoria who had been taken over by Saunders
Lerwick for munitions work, so I was directed to Kidderminster steam laundry.
I took out a driving licence and became their laundry van driver.

Melvyn Thompson's father was a loom tuner, 'but his firm was in
"mothballs" and so he joined the war effort working for the Clifford Aero
Company which had taken over Morris Carpets' premises in Hoobrook'.

June Dowe's two sisters were weavers at Tomkinsons when the factory was
changed over to munitions:

They worked there filling phosphorus bombs which had to be handled under
water. My elder sister was burned by phosphorus when a bomb was handed to
her with the top not on properly; she had a scar the size of a small plate for the
rest of her life. Both my sisters then went off to the Hartlebury Depot. The
depot supplied spares and equipment all over England. Planes would be waiting
on the ground for essential parts which needed to be delivered urgently.
Massive lorries called Queen Marys were used, and it was amazing to see them
negotiating the Kidderminster streets. When my sisters arrived at work there
was often an urgent signal such as '20 AOG', meaning 20 aircraft on the
ground awaiting spares. They liked to think they helped keep the RAF flying.

Tomkinsons' war effort included the manufacture of 4,596,882 three-inch and
336,069 four-and-a-half inch mortar bombs using 4,500 tons of
phosphorus. They also made aircraft fuel tanks and bullets.

Jessie Maskell was an Axminster weaver at Tomkinsons but, when war
started, was sent with others to Allbright & Wilson, in Oldbury. 'They were

making pellets there and I packed them. The pellets were shaped like a slice off a large white waxy candle; I believe they were phosphorus. They said they "caught fire" as they fell. We spent a lot of time in shelters because of the air raids and eventually I was moved back with Allbright & Wilson to Tomkinsons to work in the "Bomb Shop" filling mortar bombs with phosphorus.'

Working in the Bomb Shop wasn't pleasant and was mainly done by women. 'We had rubber gloves but no masks or washing facilities. Your face and hands glowed in the dark. There were a lot of girls who had chest problems afterwards, although the nurse examined us every three months.'

Jessie goes on to describe the process:

Two men kept the bosh (a large 3ft deep lead-lined water tank) supplied with bomb canisters (about 2ft of water ensured that the canisters were wet). Wet canisters were carried to a canopy-covered area and filled with phosphorus piped from a stored supply. Mr Pearsall and Mr Bayliss kept the phosphorus flowing. Filling was controlled with a hand-operated tap. When full, the canister was moved aside, the rim painted with red lead, and a cap screwed on the top. Excess phosphorus was removed by washing and the bomb placed

Some of the items manufactured by Tomkinsons during the Second World War: aircraft fuel tanks, and three- and four-and-a-half-inch phosphorus-filled mortar bombs. (*Archive Collection of the Carpet Museum*)

Tomkinsons 'Bomb Shop' workers, who filled mortar bombs with phosphorus. Jessie Maskell (née Hatton) is seen third row back, second from right, next to her friend Agnes Jennings. Seated are: Mr Booth, Herbert Tomkinson and Graham Hall (second, third and fourth from left); Sir Geoffrey Tomkinson (second from right). Gerald Tomkinson is in the second row, seventh from left. Others pictured include: Cath Bennett, Sid Cooke, Edna Evans, Nellie Gee, Alice Hatton, Alf Mason, Alf Roberts. Mr Pearsall is next to Mr Bayliss (back row, far right). *(Jessie Maskell)*

on a conveyor belt for transport to the packing section at the other end of the workshop. I worked on the four-and-a-half inch bombs.

Tomkinsons was also a major manufacturer of bullets. When still a schoolgirl Margaret Phelan had experience of bullet-making.

Girls over 15 at the High School were asked to help with an emergency: a huge consignment of small bullet sleeves had been made with too narrow a bore-hole. We were to work four-hour shifts on Saturdays at Tomkinsons, using lathes to hollow them out just a little to increase the bore. And we were going to get what seemed to us quite good pay. The fingers of your left hand, which was going to hold the bullet, were bound with sticking plaster. You held the bullet and put the sleeve on to the reamer; a foot-switch controlled whether it was spinning or not. A measure was put inside the sleeve to see whether the bore was wide enough. You were paid according to the number you did. It went on for two or three months; it was very exciting work!' Margaret kept one of the bullet sleeves as a souvenir.

Monica Hill was 16 in 1944 when she heard, on the wireless, about jobs as laboratory assistants with the Ministry of Supply:

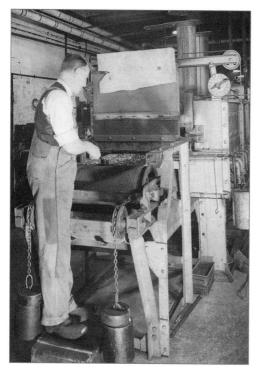

Small bullet case; a souvenir of Margaret Phelan's war work. *(Margaret Phelan)*

Bullet-making at Tomkinsons. Note the clogs. *(Archive Collection of the Carpet Museum)*

Three of us from the High School went for a three-week training course at the Leas School in Cambridge. This had been taken over, and the boys moved away. The Ministry of Supply had the school laboratories. We were allowed home at weekends. On one trip home we changed trains at Liverpool Street station and, while we sat in the train, the sirens went. We were stuck there praying that there weren't going to be any Doodlebugs. The train was absolutely packed and we sat and sang all night braving the raid out until the 'All clear' went. Quite an adventure for a teenager.

I was sent to the Queen Elizabeth's Hospital, Birmingham, where the Ministry of Supply had taken over a laboratory. I wasn't there long before they closed down and I got a job in the laboratory at Baldwin's Steel Works in Clensmore. That was a happy place. There were few young females but all the men in the factory were very kind to us and there was a real family atmosphere. I went there just before Christmas 1944 and was working on VE and VJ days. That winter was horribly cold. The canal froze over and some colleagues rode their bikes on the canal rather than on the towpath. You had to negotiate horses on the towpath as there were still horse-drawn boats then.

When Peter Carter left school he joined the Post Office Telephones as a trainee. 'We used to go out to Park Attwood which was the BBC News Centre where all foreign war correspondence and world news came. So we often knew what next day's news bulletin was going to be.

'We also went to the Rover company at Drakelow. About 300 yards down a long tunnel there was an Irish security guard. He knew you if you'd been before. I was apprenticed to a bloke called Diaper who lived up Leswell Lane. "Morning Mr Diaper, I see you've brought the big lad with you today," the guard would say.'

As the war progressed the labour force was supplemented by Italian and German prisoners of war.

Margaret Phelan recalls that 'after Italy surrendered we had Italian prisoners billeted at the Shrubbery in Birmingham Road. They worked on farms or did other labouring work during the day, but they were free enough in the evenings. I used to play tennis with friends in Brinton Park and we'd often have a group of Italian POWs watching and cheering if somebody made a good shot. They became quite a familiar sight.'

Towards the end of the war Ken Rudd's father, George Francis, worked for Boswell Contracting Company on the preparations for building the Birchen Coppice housing estate:

My Dad was one of about six or seven English foremen each supervising ten to fifteen German POW labourers working on the sewerage installations. They used small mechanical diggers to dig trenches, which were reinforced with wooden slats to stop them caving in before the pipes were laid. There were difficulties with language and it often took some time to explain exactly what had to be done. The pipes were laid in sections and tested for leaks before the trenches were filled in. The POWs were considered to be very good workers and they used to carve beautiful toys. Their camp was off Woodbury Road behind (to the west of) Jubilee Drive, where the houses around Dowles Road now stand. That camp was later expanded and used to house Irish labourers working at the sugar beet factory.

The first mention of plans for the Birchen Coppice housing estate in the Town Council Minutes was as early as 3 February 1943. An application for a '60-year loan for buildings, sewers and roads' was recorded on 20 March 1945. By 13 June 1945 '40% of the total length of water pipe' had been laid, and the first house was completed on 1 May 1946.

Many workers from outside Kidderminster were directed to the town to help with manufacturing munitions, building works or service provision. These people required accommodation which was provided in hostels or by billeting.

Margaret Phelan recalls that early in the war the basement of Birmingham Road Methodist Church was used to house a large group of Irish labourers. 'The church was next door to my mother's bungalow. Mother had given permission for them to be fed at the Borough Restaurant, where she was supervisor at the time, and other people stepped in to provide breakfast and evening meals. They were there for probably several months. What conditions were like I don't know. On Friday pay-nights, we used to get some wandering round the side of our house instead of going to the church. Even now I can hear my mother saying: "Be off!" Not to come here.'

The Carters in Larches Road hosted many people throughout the war.

> For quite a while we had a gentleman called Mr Burrows who was one of the civil engineers for the tunnels at Drakelow. At the time he couldn't tell us what he was doing and we couldn't ask; we knew he was doing something very secret. We also had a family called Fischer. He had been a newspaper editor in Sudetenland, Czechoslovakia, and had written rather rude things about Herr Hitler; so they had to get out in a hurry. He was working at the sugar beet factory. Another man who stayed was Mr Samways, who had worked in "sugar" in the Far East and had been allocated to Kidderminster. We always had more than a houseful and often the visitors overlapped.

Sheila Kirk's family in Baldwin Road had a woman lodger from Smethwick in the front room. Her firm had evacuated to Adams' factory on Birmingham Road. 'She kept strictly to herself and didn't eat with us. She was fearsome and dour; probably wasn't very old but seemed like it. Complained about me singing and laughing; did she fear I was laughing at her? But I was only 6 or 7 and in bed by 7 p.m. Mercifully, she went home at weekends. We all breathed a sigh of relief when she went back to Smethwick for good.'

In industrial towns throughout the country there were many people employed on essential defence work away from home and this threw a burden on local catering facilities. Early on, the government decreed that councils should establish communal restaurants to provide nourishing meals for these workers. Mostly, these restaurants were under central direction but locally the Borough Council stayed in control via the Communal Food Committee headed by Mr L. Tolley.

An account of the opening of the first such restaurant in Kidderminster on Wednesday 16 April was in the *Shuttle* the following Saturday: 'Instead of the customary sharp medical smells that normally hover over a clinic there was a new odorous scent of steak & kidney pie in the clinic in Prospect Lane. The food was beautifully cooked and a choice could be made of steak & kidney pie, cabbage and potatoes (8*d*), steamed pudding and custard (3*d*), fish cakes (4*d*), pasties (4*d*), bread (1*d*) or tea (1*d*). For the present the restaurant will open for lunch only from 12.30 p.m. to 2 p.m. A sit-down meal will be provided but food may be purchased at the handsome counter and taken away.' A second restaurant was opened in November 1941 in the Salvation Army Citadel, Dudley Street.

Margaret Phelan's mother, Mrs A. Pugh, worked in the Prospect Lane Borough Restaurant as cook supervisor until it closed down in 1950.

The building was of corrugated iron and the main room was provided with trestle tables and wooden benches. The diners paid a cashier (Mrs Vial) as they came in and received tear-off tickets. At peak times over 300 meals were served by WVS volunteers every weekday. Mother kept many of her records of that time. The kitchen was to the rear of the dining area. It would not

Mrs Pugh's notebook, detailing meals produced in 1950 at the Kidderminster Borough Restaurant. *(Margaret Phelan)*

have been condemned today; it would never have been allowed to open. In summer time the temperature reached over 100°F and in winter it was sub-zero until the fires warmed the place. Freddie, the Council handyman often had to deal with frozen pipes, electricity failures, rats and mice and a leaking roof.

Hot water came from a large gas-heated steamer; there were two or three gas stoves for cooking and a gas-heated hot plate where food was dished up onto the plates. Typical menus included shepherd's pie, brown stew, roast meat, corned beef hash and cheese pie. Sweets were mainly jam tart, steam pudding or fruit and custard and were prepared by Mrs Phyl Coles. Semolina with a dribble of jam was also popular.

There was nothing stylish, people were not encouraged to sit and talk; it was just a place where you went and had a good meal. But it was very popular. Mother left when the restaurant closed down in 1950; she had several letters of appreciation for all the work she had done.

Military personnel generally had their own catering arrangements, but for those not so well served a canteen was opened in Orchard Street by Monica Hill's mother, Nell Carter. 'Mom joined the WVS and one job she had was starting a YMCA canteen for servicemen. It was an awful dump; an old carpet warehouse. Nothing was issued; they had to "beg, borrow or steal" furniture, crockery, cutlery, and so on. Eventually they did get a small ration allowance for making tea and sandwiches. Nowadays it would be considered so primitive, but then they were only too glad to have anything.'

Local people and 'guest' workers had an intense working life throughout the war. They contributed in so many ways to the nation's war effort. Whether as armament workers, skilled or unskilled, military personnel, housewives, providers of food or lodgings, schoolchildren or POWs – all were involved. We were fortunate, for a town so involved with armament and munitions work, that we were able to 'get on with the job' without the substantial disruption arising from the air-raid devastation that affected so many other industrialised towns and cities.

The importance of our being able and willing to 'do our bit' is reflected in a report to Congress by President Roosevelt: 'The Eighth Army captured some cans. They were sent back to England and the British started manufacturing them. They were called "Jerricans". Many millions of these cans were filled and ready to go on D-Day. They were amongst the first supplies landed on the beaches of France. Without these cans it would have been impossible for our armies to cut their way across France at a lightning pace.'

A tribute to the 'Brintons' jerrican.

7

SHORTAGES AND RATIONING

Some of the most common memories of the Second World War are associated with shortages of commodities – particularly food. Imported foodstuff became scarce, and British farmers helped by producing record amounts. Extra land was 'put to the plough' and scarce agricultural labour supplemented by a female organisation: the Land Army. Locally, some flat areas of the golf course off Barnett's Lane were cultivated by Land Army women.

Nevertheless, the government intervened to supervise food production and distribution to ensure that the population had an adequate diet.

All food was subject to control but the basic foods of meat, cheese, cooking fats, milk, sugar, jam, tea, eggs and sweets were strictly rationed. Ministry of Food experts advised the government on suitable diets and in the autumn of 1939 everyone was issued with a ration book containing coupons to exchange when goods on the ration list were purchased.

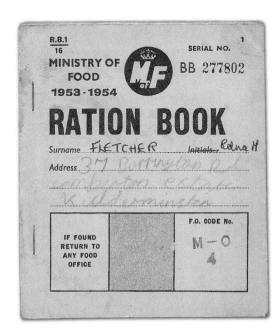

A post-war ration book for 1953–4 issued in Kidderminster. *(Edna Fletcher)*

MINISTRY OF FOOD

REGISTRATION

for

BACON & HAM • BUTTER • SUGAR

All ration books have now been posted, and all members of the public should register with their shopkeepers for Bacon & Ham, Butter and Sugar before

Thursday, 23rd November

Registration is a necessary measure to ensure adequate supplies and fair distribution. It is essential to the smooth working of food distribution in war-time.

SIMPLE INSTRUCTIONS FOR YOUR GUIDANCE

1 Put your name and address at the bottom of the Bacon & Ham, Butter and Sugar pages of your Ration Book *NOW*.

2 Write on page II (The inside cover of your Ration Book) the name and address of your shopkeeper for each of the three foods—*Bacon, Butter and Sugar*.

3 Take your Ration Book to your shopkeepers for Bacon & Ham, Butter and Sugar.

4 Let the shopkeepers write their names and addresses on the appropriate counterfoils and cut them out.

5 The numbered coupons should not be cut out yet. This will be done by the shopkeepers when rationing begins.

6 Only the pages for Bacon & Ham, Butter and Sugar are to be used. You should *not* register for any other food.

7 Although the page for Butter includes Margarine ignore this, as Margarine is not being rationed.

8 Sugar is not being rationed at present, but registration is necessary.

9 If you change your address, take your Ration Book to the Local Food Officer in your new district.

10 Don't forget that you are free to choose your own shopkeepers.

A SHOPKEEPER WILL ONLY BE ABLE TO GET SUPPLIES FOR HIS REGISTERED CUSTOMERS

REGISTER NOW

AN ANNOUNCEMENT BY THE MINISTRY OF FOOD, GT. WESTMINSTER HOUSE, LONDON. S W.

Poster issued in autumn 1939 providing essential information about rationing procedures. (*Godfrey Jones*)

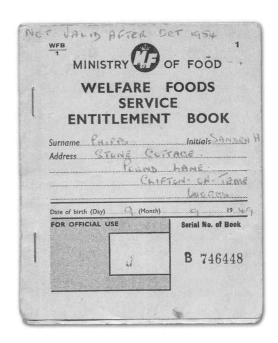

Locally issued Welfare Foods Book for
1954, entitling children to special foods.
(Joan Phipps)

A notice was issued by the Ministry of Food confirming that ration books had
been posted to everybody and registration with shopkeepers was now necessary.

Welfare Foods booklets gave children access to special foods, such as orange
juice, rosehip syrup and cod liver oil.

Food rationing began in January 1940. The food allowed was minimal: it
would be considered scarcely adequate today. The weekly butter ration of 2oz
per adult would make few sandwiches, and housewives struggled to cook
nourishing meals with only 4oz of cooking fat.

Sausages were not rationed but were difficult to obtain. Food rationing was
not abandoned until long after the war was over, meat being the last food to be
de-rationed, in 1954.

Ann Mole recalls: 'Food wasn't too scarce at first but later shortages really
began to bite. There were always plenty of vegetables and fruit – especially
from local farmers – but other things were in short supply. The nicer or more
unusual items were often not available at all. Rice remained difficult to get until
1948. I was once asked what I would like for a treat: my answer was "rice
pudding!" Rations were supplemented by growing our own vegetables. I think
we had enough to eat, but food certainly wasn't plentiful – particularly meat.'

Mrs Jackson remembers: 'Food was scarce and when shops had a delivery
word got round and queues formed very quickly. I remember my mother
queuing for ages at MacFisheries; she had no idea what she would get. She'd
heard that fresh fish was available and it was too good a chance to miss.'

Table 4. *The basic ration permitted for adults*

Foodstuff	Quantity per week, unless stated otherwise	Rationing began in
Bacon and ham	4oz	January 1940
Meat	To the value of 1s 2d	March 1940
Butter	2oz	January 1940
Cheese	2oz, but sometimes 4oz or more	July 1940
Margarine	4oz	July 1940
Cooking fat	4oz, but often only 2oz	July 1940
Milk	3 pints, but sometimes only 2 pints, plus 'Household' dried milk: about 1 packet every 4 weeks	November 1941
Sugar	8oz	January 1940
Jam, marmalade, etc.	1lb every 2 months	March 1941
Tea	2oz	July 1940
Eggs	1 shell egg per week. If unavailable, 1 per fortnight. Plus 1 packet of dried eggs every 4 weeks	June 1941
Sweets	12oz every 4 weeks	July 1942

On the same theme, June Dowe had similar experiences. 'We were in Marks and Spencer's when my mother saw people gathering. "Look out, there's something coming," she said; so we formed a queue. Eventually a shop girl came out with jellies which were not easily got hold of. We were allowed one jelly.'

Alf Mole's mother eked out their meagre fuel allowance by co-operation with neighbours. 'We had a bathroom, whereas most people had a tin bath. Neighbours used to say "Here's a bucket of coal, Mrs Mole, can my two have a bath?" It helped to keep our house warm and heat the water. A black line was painted on the bath to show how much water was allowed. The more children in the bath the higher the water came!'

Sheila Kirk recalls many facets of rationing that, as a child growing up during the Second World War, she took for granted:

Sheward's farm shop was kept by Granny Roberts, a tiny bent old lady. At the beginning of the war I went for some apples, and she gave me a banana, saying: 'Make it last, there won't be any more till the war's over.' I think that we had to register for some foodstuffs at specific shops. For butter we were 'rationed' at the Co-op at Greenhill. A large slab of butter sat on the counter and the grocer weighed the amount allowed. Ditto the cheese. Most of our bread came from Howell's in Hurcott Road. Threepence threefarthings for a small batch, and fourpence halfpenny for a large white. Earlier Mother had worked for Howell's, but we weren't given special treatment. Mum would often say, 'After all I did for them!' Once I waited ages for a penny bar of Cadbury's chocolate, and a penn'orth of raspberry drops in a cone of white paper due in at the sweetshop in the Horsefair. On summer Sunday mornings my Grandad brought us a special treat from his garden – a stick of rhubarb tucked into a blue sugar bag. We dipped and sucked with relish. People were always chivvying us with the adage: 'There's a war on! Waste not want not' – or worse still: 'There's many a starving prisoner would be glad to eat that!'

There was some scheme whereby extra essentials were given out at school. Occasionally we received a tin of blackcurrant purée or a tin of jam, an orange or apple. Several times we had cocoa powder in a little twist of paper. These never got home!

Rationing was supposed to even out the supply of food so that distribution wasn't abused. However, there were various lawful ways round the system. Mrs Jackson again: 'Lots of families helped each other trading food coupons. For instance, if a person didn't like margarine they might swap their sugar ration for butter.'

Food coupons were a valuable commodity and anyone not needing their full quota could always find a willing buyer. This wasn't approved officially but it certainly was not uncommon, as recalled by June Dowe.

Everybody had a ration book. I don't think we can appreciate the difficulties our parents had making ends meet. We didn't have a lot of money, but we did have three wages coming into the house. Occasionally, someone selling food coupons would knock at the door. It wasn't legal but it helped poorer people in need of money; I suppose it was a form of black market. Probably my mother did this to get us a few treats. When my mother was spreading something on a slice of bread I would say: "I hope that isn't that horrible margarine", which was yellow, hard and greasy. So I expect she wanted extra coupons to get me a bit of butter, or something like that.

Of course, imported foods were scarce; a generation of children was born who had never seen a banana. Mrs Jackson's brother, Raymond Badger, who was aged 4 towards the end of the war, was one. 'Our parents managed to buy two bananas and put them in the pantry overnight. I was so fascinated by those bananas that I slipped downstairs and ate one.' The following morning his mother asked sternly: 'Did you steal a banana?' When he confessed, she asked how he liked it and he replied: 'It was lovely – but the skin wasn't half tough!'

Melvyn Thompson was another not impressed with bananas. 'The first time I saw a banana I was 7 years old. My best friend John Hanglin had an auntie who was the town clerk's secretary and it may have been her who obtained this peculiar shaped yellow and brown object. Our gang gathered round as it was cut into pieces for us to taste. I think we all agreed it was not very nice and bananas would never catch on!'

He also remembers how differently food was marketed. 'The milkman came with a churn and ladled a pint into the jug that had been left for him. The bread man came with a wickerwork basket, always just as I was going to bed. He walked into the house through the back door – it was never locked.' He recalls:

> Midday 'dinner' was our main meal. We had potatoes, peas and beans from our garden; the small orchard at the top provided apples and damsons. A joint of rationed meat, such as it was, provided Sunday dinner. Monday was washing day, and we ate the leftovers; anything remaining after that was turned into rissoles. Occasionally my dad would be given a rabbit, which helped a lot. Mother always made sure we cleaned our plates and at the end of the meal she would say 'Hitler can have what I've left!'
>
> The big treat after Sunday lunch was the weekly piece of Cadbury's milk chocolate bought with sweet coupons. Sweets were rationed and this continued long after the end of the war. The first day sweets came off ration was a Sunday; after morning service at St George's I cycled at top speed to the corner shop in Lorne Street to join the queue. But when I got there they had sold out. I felt I had to buy something so I got a tin of Zubes.

One way to avoid the more acute aspects of food shortages was to be part of the supply chain. One gentleman remembers: 'We kept a grocer's shop in Hurcott Road and as a result we didn't experience any real shortage. My job was to collect the coupons from customers by clipping them out of their ration books. We then entered the details on a form which I took to the wholesaler every week.'

The government recognised that many people would attempt to become more self-sufficient and, while encouraging this in respect of egg production and the growing of fruit and vegetables, it insisted that a proportion of meat produced by individuals be placed in the national food chain. Thus pigs and other livestock raised in gardens and on smallholdings were supposed to be shared with the rest of the population. One former smallholder remembers the phrase 'One pig for us, one for the government'.

Food for pigs was collected from leftover scraps. Mrs Jackson has distinct memories of this. 'Pig bins were in many streets in Kidderminster, often under lamp-posts or in other prominent positions, and people would add spare scraps of food. These were supposed to be collected regularly but the smell was very unpleasant, sometimes made worse by scavenging dogs knocking the bins over to get at the food.'

Monica Hill's family also had pigs and chickens. 'The pigs were shared with a neighbour who had an empty garage where the pigs were kept. Neighbours brought their pig swill to us. When the fatal day came, of course, they expected a few slices of bacon. We kept well away when the slaughter man came. We became very fond of one pair of saddle back pigs which were very tame and we didn't keep any more after those. My mother said "it was like eating the family".'

Meat was in particularly short supply. 'My grandparents lived at Dunley and were very poor,' remembers Roy Bayliss. 'They poached rabbits or pheasants and passed some on to us. We virtually lived off rabbits in the war. A lady living in Heightington came round the village every week on an old sit-up-and-beg bicycle; strung across the handlebars were lots of rabbits for sale to help out with the meat rations.'

Alf Mole's father had a rabbit shoot round his area. 'They never shot them; they always netted them so the animal wasn't damaged by pellets splintering the bone. They used to go rabbiting every other week. Their area was from Offmore Farm along the Birmingham Road to Blakedown and right across to the Hagley/Worcester Road. A lot of people would have gone hungry without those rabbits.'

The phrase 'Dig for Victory' was coined by the government to encourage as much fruit and vegetable production as possible. A chart was issued showing how to plant various crops at different times to produce fresh vegetables virtually all year round. 'Our allotments helped to ease the food shortages,' said Les Lench. 'We had two allotments on Greatfield Road where we grew a lot of our own food; although we were encouraged to do this by the government it was largely self-preservation in our case. We had a big family of eleven to feed when everybody was at home. My dad and uncles kept pigs and exchanged bacon for things like sugar. It was a bit like the old barter system. There was the odd bit of dishonesty around. I remember the story about one man who was pilfering where he worked at the sugar beet factory: he would fill his bike frame with sugar. He became greedy and was caught when walking out with his wellingtons full of sugar.'

Roy Bayliss remembers other ways in which people tried to cheat the system:

My first job was for the Severn & Canal Carrying Company. On their Nelson Wharf, down towards Lincomb, they handled food – butter, cheese, condensed milk and the like – all the rationed foods. Food would be unloaded from barges and lorries would take it to holding depots. My job as office boy was checking goods as they came in. On one occasion I had to go to Nelson Wharf to examine some tinned salmon which the bargees claimed was blown. There were holes in the top of each can in two or three crates. I reported this to the foreman at the other wharf who came to see. Later on he said to me, 'We've opened one of the tins and it looks all right. Would you like one to take home?' It turned out that the bargees had punched holes in some of the tins expecting them to be condemned so they could sell them at the Severn Trow and other pubs in Stourport. When I got home and offered my mother this tin of salmon she was furious and very suspicious. 'You take it back,' she said. 'Everything's on ration.' But eventually she relented and we kept it.

A similar kind of deceit was tried with cheese. 'I was asked to check off cheeses which were being delivered. These round cheeses were as big as a bicycle wheel and being loaded from the hold onto a crane skip to be hoisted to the wharf. I heard a shout and the man in the hold asked the foreman to look at a cheese at the bottom of the stack. We went down and saw that the bottom of the cheese had been cut away and most of the middle removed, leaving just the outer skin. Unscrupulous bargees must have stolen it. This was regarded as very serious and the manager was fetched.'

June Dowe's father was a good gardener and regularly supplemented their food with produce grown in his allotments. 'He brought vegetables home in his wheelbarrow and arranged the best on the top, so that as he passed the big houses on Birmingham Road people could see how good they were.'

Mike Compton's family was one of many who did not have the good fortune of an allotment. 'We couldn't grow much in our garden at Abberley because the soil was poor. Food was difficult – but we did have a good relationship with the local farmer and we could get goods off the farm. Of course, we had to do it secretly as all food was earmarked for proper distribution. We had cracked eggs and skimmed milk – and a bit of butter in the milk made it like normal. We got a special sort of margarine with the coupons and used to have sugar sandwiches. Jam was scarce and when the pot was nearly empty my brothers would fight over who got the jam jar. They used to put a bit of bread on a fork and clean it out.'

Some landowners were able to set up their own sources of food. One evacuee remembers being billeted on such a family. He duly submitted his ration book to them which gave an entitlement to one egg a week. 'I was amazed to see that this didn't apply there and the family's retriever gundogs had six eggs a day.'

Before the availability of freezers it was difficult to keep food for long periods, but Jackie Bayliss recalls how some foods were preserved in Areley Kings:

There was a Canning Club, which met in the parish rooms where local ladies canned jam and fruit. They used produce from their own gardens and the cans and tops came from the Metal Box Company at Worcester. They hired equipment from Metal Box and used the gas boiler to sterilise the tins. The food was mainly for themselves, but they gave any surplus away to less fortunate people in the village. It must have been quite a sociable occasion when the club met. There was a notice board outside the parish rooms advertising the club meetings. One day Mrs Speke's husband altered the word 'canning' to 'canting' – no explanation necessary.

We always tried to help each other out in the war. If my mum had spare food coupons she would give them to a neighbour who had a bigger family and was always short. In those days whatever you had to spare you shared with neighbours. My dad gave lots of vegetables away and never charged a penny. He put the garden down to vegetables and wouldn't have a lawn. 'You can't eat grass,' he said.

It was not only food which was rationed; there were shortages generally as more and more domestic production was turned over to war work.

Torch batteries were in short supply. Most people carried a torch to negotiate the blackout. 'If the rumour got round that a shop had a stock of batteries in, long queues would form to buy them,' says Margaret Phelan. 'I'm afraid that some unscrupulous dealers collected old batteries, warmed them up in the oven for a bit to revive them temporarily, and sold them. There were a lot of get-rich-quick fixes like that during the war when the "wide boys" got going.'

Supplies could be a problem. On Friday 12 December 1941 milk had not been delivered to St George's Junior School for more than a week, and in the midst of a heavy snowfall in January 1945 there was only enough heating fuel left for one day.

Clothing in particular was controlled and coupons were issued early in the war. Many women remember that 'there never seemed to be enough clothing coupons'; and although certain items – in particular work clothes, baby clothes, sewing materials, haberdashery and clogs – were not rationed, normal clothing remained controlled until 1949. As the war progressed the demand for textiles to make uniforms increased and fewer and fewer clothing coupons were issued. From an already low base, coupons fell to 48 per person per year by 1943; and in 1945 there were only 36 for each person.

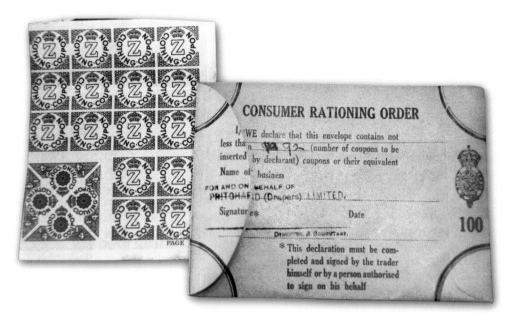

Exchanged clothing coupons ready to be sent off by Pritchard's drapers shop. *(Pritchard's, late of Oxford Street)*

As Table 5 (page 91) shows, those quantities would not go very far for a young woman wanting to look her best.

Men's clothing was similarly subject to control, but with so many men in the forces, or other uniformed organisations, their needs were not always such a problem.

Shopkeepers were required to account and sign for coupons collected in exchange for goods. Pritchard's drapers shop in Kidderminster must have done this on a regular basis.

With new clothing being scarce people made do with what was available. One of the fabrics not rationed was material for lining and making blackout curtains. This was used by enterprising mothers to make clothes for their children, as was parachute material whenever it became available. 'Supplies of clothing were short. We made ours from parachute material,' says one mother. 'We would fit the pattern to the panels. Parachutes had different colours, depending on what was being dropped, and that was the colour of our clothes.' Other schemes to eke out the meagre fabric allowance were devised: 'We economised on clothing, unpicking items and re-making them. We cut sheets down the middle and turned them sides to middle so that they could be re-used.'

Table 5. *Number of coupons needed for items of clothing*

Item of clothing	Women	Girls
Macintosh or coat over 28 inches	14	11
Short coat or jacket under 28 inches	11	8
Wool dress	11	8
Dress of other fabric	7	5
Skirt or gym tunic	8	6
Blouse, shirt, jumper or cardigan	5	3
Pyjamas	8	6
Nightdress	6	5
Slippers, boots or shoes	5	3
Petticoat, slip or cami knickers	4	3
Scarf, gloves or mittens	2	2
Pair of stockings	2	1
Wool cloth 36 x 36 inches	3	3
Knitting wool (2oz)	1	1

'New clothes carried the "Utility" mark as a sign of a fairly basic approved quality level,' remembers Melvyn Thompson. 'But most of my clothes were hand-me-downs from my brother. In those days all lads wore short trousers held up by braces. When I joined the choir my dad bought me a suit with long trousers from the Fifty Shilling Tailors in Vicar Street, near the town hall – I hated it.'

Footwear in particular was scarce. Children had to make do with fewer coupons, but occasionally children who were well grown would receive extra if their feet were approaching adult size. This was sometimes decided by measurements in schools, with pupils standing between two chalked lines. For the poorer families the local police ran a charity. Les Lench recalls: 'My clothing throughout the war was basically a pair of police boots, a pair of trousers and a jersey. Police boots were supplied to poor families.

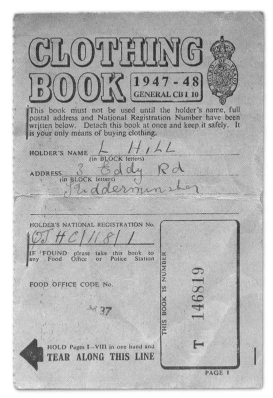

A Kidderminster issued clothing book of coupons for 1947–48. *(Edna Fletcher)*

You went to the police station and a pair of boots was issued. The police punched holes in the uppers so that people couldn't sell them. One family cut off the top part of the boots to remove the holes and make them look like shoes – and then sold them. When I went for my boots my Dad told me to wear two pairs of socks so that I could get a bigger pair that would last me longer.'

The police had a fund for the relief of the poor. June Dowe: 'My father raised money in an interesting way. Every year we had a Christmas tree set in a box, like a tea chest, big enough to hold a model farm scene made out of lead – the farmhouse, an old couple on a bench, various animals, a hen laying eggs, a road with a motorbike and a policeman. It was very attractive. Children were encouraged to come and play with it and my father charged them a penny. He gave all the money he collected to the Police Fund for the poor.'

In the 1940s there were no such things as nylon tights. Women wishing to be well dressed wore silk stockings. Unfortunately, these were almost unobtainable as silk production was needed for making parachutes and women made do with various alternatives. One popular solution was a dye which tinted legs to the colour of stockings. This was a commercial product and if it was not available Oxo or Bisto was sometimes used instead. In those days stockings had seams at the back, so pencil or crayon lines were added to give a realistic appearance.

Many people didn't have the resources to buy extras; indeed some found it difficult to manage when they had large families. One gentleman recalls: 'There was a general shortage of clothing and it was expensive. My father had one good suit which he would pawn on Mondays and redeem it for the weekend when he got paid on Friday.'

It was difficult to obtain many items taken for granted today. In particular, soap was much sought after. Les Lench had been a breadwinner in the early part of the war and when called up it created difficulties. 'However, the family managed to save up and send some soap. I don't know where they got it from but I was the envy of the barracks. Other soldiers weren't beyond trying to steal it.'

Advertisement for a dye to imitate ladies' stockings. *(The Robert Opie Collection)*

One major shortage was petrol. In the 1940s cars were much less common than today and few people had the means to own one. Nevertheless, petrol was strictly controlled with priority given for military usage. Limited petrol coupons were issued to those owning a car and who could prove they needed it for essential work – doctors, for example.

These coupons were highly desirable and commanded a big price on the black market. Those owning a car before the war, and not meriting a petrol allowance, laid their cars up for the duration. After the war it was some time before private car production was re-established and many of these vehicles were sold for several times their original price.

Sheila Kirk says that bus transport was 'hit and miss'. 'There was an odd custom then. On half-day closing women piled off to

Home-made tommy guns for Christmas 1944. *(Bob Millward)*

the next town for a look around. I could not understand this. Often there was no bus, sometimes a train if we walked to the station first. More than once we walked halfway to Worcester or Stourbridge before a bus came along.'

There was no toy production during the war; children had to make do with home-made or renovated second-hand ones. Mike Compton must have felt particularly deprived: 'We had no toys. We used a sauce bottle as a toy bus. When we wanted a double-decker we put one sauce bottle on top of another.'

Graham Williams and his cousin Bob Millward were more fortunate by those standards. The photograph shows them with their 1944 Christmas presents. 'These tommy guns were made in Glasgow by the father of an ATS girl billeted in Kidderminster,' recollects Graham. 'The guns were wooden and a handle was turned to produce an exciting "Rat-a-tat-tat" noise made by a sprung ratchet system. I can't remember if the Scottish type forage caps came with the guns or from my dad, who was serving with the Glasgow Highlanders.'

The tommy gun was a popular item at that time as Melvyn Thompson, too, was delighted to receive one as a Christmas present. 'Toys were scarce. Dad was always the mechanic and made some extraordinary toys. One Christmas I was thrilled to receive a tommy gun made out of electrical conduit. Dad had cut a toothed wheel from a piece of wood so that when the wheel was turned a realistic sound filled the air. I couldn't wait to show the rest of my gang; but when they arrived they also had one – exactly like mine. He didn't miss a trick!

One year my brother's '0' gauge clockwork train set went missing in September – only to reappear in my stocking painted a different colour. I remember pretending to be pleased.'

Bob Millward also felt lucky to get toy soldiers. 'These were cavalry figures cast from soft metal – probably solder. They provided hours of fun and although they dented easily they stayed in one piece even after rough treatment.'

This was the age before plastic and many durable toys were made of metal. Most of the usual metals used for toy making were not available because metallurgical production was reserved for the manufacture of war materials. Scrap iron was an essential part of steel production and the government decided that as much scrap as possible should be collected. As part of the scheme people were encouraged to send in unwanted metal objects such as pans, tools and tins. One man remembers: 'I was about 8 or 9 when I went round the neighbours with my trolley and collected scrap which I think the council took away. It all went off somewhere to help with the war effort.'

Early in the drive to get as much scrap metal as possible a decision was made that all non-essential decorative ironwork should be removed from buildings. Iron railings around churchyards and schools, and from the gardens of houses, were collected on behalf of the local council – usually by men with huge shears which cut off the railings near the bottom. One Areley Kings resident recalls: 'In the village nearly every house had iron railings and these were taken away. Areley Court had a magnificent pair of wrought iron gates known as the Green Gates. They disappeared in the war and it was said that they were melted down along with the railings. After the war we heard that they were not used but were acquired by a private collector. They really were a work of art.'

Even historic artefacts were not entirely immune. An entry in the Kidderminster Town Council Minutes, March 1940, reads: 'Sale of Waste Materials. Your Committee recommends that, in view of the need for scrap iron, the tank, guns and other old war material in Brinton Park, with the exception of the old Crimean Cannon, be sold.'

One set of railings at the house of Mrs Ann Mole's parents wasn't removed. 'Our family home had an ornate iron gate, and railings round the front garden. These were all cut down and taken away. But along the side of the front garden an ordinary iron fence with spikes on top escaped this fate. Why was that? It was because Mother agreed to become a salvage warden and she hung hessian sacks on these spikes every Friday morning. People from Chester Road North put paper, cans, glass and bones into the sacks to be collected at the end of the day. The empty sacks were then put into the shed until the following week.'

Many others have spoken about salvage. 'Every Tuesday we had a load of hessian sacks hung up along our drive: one for bottles, one for cans and one for papers,' says one person. 'All the neighbours collected their stuff during the week and on salvage day emptied their bags and boxes into these sacks. They were collected in the evening and a pile of clean sacks left for the following week.'

Pam Melloy's family routinely re-used mail envelopes. At school she was encouraged to bring old books, papers and magazines for recycling. 'Depending on how much you brought, you would receive a cardboard disc bearing the rank Corporal or Sergeant or Captain to pin on your chest.'

So recycling isn't a new idea!

Despite the shortages and difficulties experienced, many people look back with mixed emotions to the times of austerity during the war; often not all memories are unpleasant. Of course, very young children had no idea of life under peacetime conditions and they made the best of things. Melvyn Thompson sums up what many people expressed: 'When I look at children these days and what they have – the toys, the endless supply of crisps and sweets, television and computers – I sometimes think back to the first eight years of my life and wonder what I would have done had things been normal. However, we made the best of it. We either walked or cycled everywhere, we made our own entertainment, we talked to each other and, more to the point, we appreciated and valued what we had. I doubt that today's children are as happy as we were in those days when the country was in the throes of war.'

8

SCHOOLDAYS AND EDUCATION

When the country became embroiled in the bitter battle with Germany in 1939 large numbers of men were required for the armed forces. Munitions work drew men, women and materials directly into the war effort as opposed to more traditional occupations and institutions. It would not have been surprising if educational developments and associated building works had ground to a halt.

This seems not to have been the case, although it is probable that the pace of progress was slowed. Thus we find that the secondary modern (senior) schools, Harry Cheshire and Sladen, were able to open in October 1940 despite the distraction of war. Before this, Kidderminster children in state education had remained in the elementary schools until the age of 14 – unless they won a scholarship to either King Charles I or Queen Elizabeth Grammar Schools (boys) or Kidderminster High School (girls). The elementary schools now became primary or junior schools and children were transferred to the senior schools at the age of 11. These developments had their roots in proposals back in the 1920s, but did not become universally established until the (Butler) Education Act of 1944. The Act also raised the school leaving age from 14 to 15 and introduced selective education between secondary modern and grammar schools by the 11+ examination.

The declaration of war had an immediate and dramatic effect on many Kidderminster schools: that of needing to provide classroom accommodation for large numbers of evacuated children and their teachers. Perhaps the effect and pressure that this put onto school accommodation can be appreciated from entries in the logbook of St George's Infant School, Leswell Street, for 1939: 'Sept 11: Re-opened school this morning after an extended holiday of five weeks, due to staff being engaged in evacuation duties. Seventy children from Brasshouse Lane Infants' School, Smethwick, have been accommodated in two class-rooms of the school, necessitating two classes having to be removed from their original rooms.'

This was in a school that had only four classrooms, four year groups and an average attendance of just over 100 at that period.

Betty Park, in her book *Horsefair and Broadwaters*, records that the children attending St Mary's Boys' School also had to 'suffer' an extra week of holiday while arrangements were made for Smethwick children.

This level of disruption did not last long when the feared air raids did not appear. A later 1939 entry in the St George's logbook records: '20 Nov: The remainder of the Smethwick evacuees (21 in number) were absorbed into this department today and placed in the correct classes according to age. The teaching is left to the staff of this school – none of the Smethwick teachers remaining in the school, for teaching purposes.'

So, school life went on little changed and we hear, for example, of quite normal Christmas celebrations: 'Wed 21 Dec 1939: At 2.15 this afternoon a Christmas concert of Carols, songs, recitation and a play were performed. The Vicar in charge, Revd P.J. Martin, distributed toys, chocolate and mince pies to the children. Miss Evans and Miss Lewis, representing the Smethwick evacuees, were also present.'

But further regular and irregular incursions into the school day were to come: gas mask testing and air-raid practices and alerts. Alf Mole remembers doing lessons at Lea Street school in a gas mask, sometimes for an hour; 'after an hour you were soaked with sweat'. Invariably, either air-raid practices or air-raid alerts meant a trip to the shelter. Many schools had their own shelter built in the school grounds. That in St George's Infant School was in the corner of the playground nearest to Offmore Road. (Former pupils remember this being demolished by Italian prisoners of war – probably in 1945 or 1946.) The school repaired to this shelter on some twenty occasions when siren-led air-raid alerts occurred; and for occasional practice.

An example in 1941: 'Nov 28: A warning siren was heard at 3.58. Just as the children were about to be dismissed they were taken to the shelter, where the majority of them remained until the "All clear" at 4.43. Rev. P.J. Martin was present in the shelter for part of the time.'

Sheila Kirk (née Ryder) was a pupil who used this shelter:

We did frequent drills, but never had to use them for real, as far as I can remember. At the given signal of the bell, we lined up in classes and silently followed Miss across the yard wearing gas masks – we would have been sitting ducks in an attack. I remember two boys being sent back into school on their own for talking (6-year-olds, can you imagine that today?) and was petrified for them, because, as small children, we thought it was for real. There was a Union Jack flag in there and some emergency stores such as water and maybe biscuits; we did not sample them. The shelter was quite dry; we sat on the concrete floor and we sang patriotic songs and had stories and word games. If you needed the toilet, too bad. You had to wait. Of course, it was pitch dark in there, but I think candles were lit, or an oil lamp. What a fire risk. There were buckets of sand dotted about, for the smothering of fires.

Not all schools were so well provided, especially the rural ones. Mike Compton recalls: 'At Abberley school we dug slit trenches in the school yard in case of air raids – one for the girls and one for the boys. It's a good job that we never had to use them because for most of the time they were full of water.'

At first, St George's Junior School in Offmore Road used nearby makeshift shelter accommodation: Ruth Rudd's class used a cellar in a cobbler's shop on the corner of George Street and South Street. The shoe repairer was a Mr Hardiman, a busy man who wore a built-up boot. Other classes used different facilities including the cellars of the Royal Oak. The school was, however, equipped with four electric lamps and three torches for use in those shelters. Eventually, a purpose-built shelter was erected in the playground behind the outdoor lavatories sometime in 1943.

Perhaps St Mary's Boys' School also relied on non-school shelter facilities because in 1940 the headmaster complained that there was no proper exit from the air-raid shelter at the Royal George (Hall Street); probably they also made use of the cellar in the Sailor's Return in Duke Place.

However, this was better protection than existed at Areley Common school. One ex-pupil remembers: 'If the sirens went we had to go into the cloakroom and hide under our coats! We had no shelters at school. Later in the war two were built on the Dunley Road, but they were mainly for the residents.'

Bill Bury describes his experiences at the Sladen School: 'When air-raid drills were carried out, we filed into the specially constructed shelters built in the quadrangle. Occasionally, gas masks would be worn.'

We know that Harry Cheshire School also had shelters because the *Kidderminster Shuttle* of 22 February 1941 reported a discussion about whether sufficient shelter protection was provided for the 200 evacuated children from Clacton, as well as 700 Kidderminster scholars.

Trenches were dug on the playing fields of King Charles I Grammar School in 1938 when war was first threatened, and filled in again after the Munich agreement, only to be excavated again in 1939.

The Lea Street school shelters were too small according to Alf Mole: 'At the back of the school, near the boiler, were some big arches and a brick wall leading from the playground to Lea Street. Older children were sent to stand against the wall or under the arches. We had an air-raid shelter but it wasn't big enough for us all. It was well disciplined. There was no hesitation; when you were told to go, you went. I only remember doing that sort of thing about three times.'

The Girls' High School was strict, well organised and supportive. Margaret Phelan was in the lower fourth when war broke out. 'We were all very apprehensive and equipped with gas masks. You were sent home if you got to school without your gas mask; you had to go and get it. We also practised what to do when the air-raid sirens went; some of us had to go through a little gate in a high wall into the cellars of Hill Grove House. We were given barley sugars to suck, so we didn't mind that. Fortunately for us there weren't too many air-raid warnings during the daytime; but senior girls were also organised to do fire watching and first-aid duties.'

Ann Mole was also a pupil at the High School and remembers the cellars. 'The house belonged to the Dudleys and we could get two forms into the cellars – up to sixty of us.'

Other educational changes were to affect the Infant and Junior schools as a result of opening the Harry Cheshire and Sladen schools in 1940. Instead of staying at junior school until they were 14, pupils now moved to one of these senior schools at the age of 11; so there was spare capacity. At St George's Junior School the upper floor remained closed for a year and furniture was taken to the Sladen School. Gradually the junior school filled up again: the 7-8 year group (Standard I) was transferred permanently from the infant school in August 1941 – with their teacher, Miss Southall. Additionally, for the first time since 1912, the children emerging from Class I (6- to 7-year-olds) were also transferred. The junior school was eventually brought to full strength (then 230) by transferring 102 children, plus furniture, from Coventry Street School when that was closed in the summer of 1942.

A wartime innovation, established by the local education service, was the introduction of school meals at lunchtime. These were prepared and sent out from newly installed kitchens in what had been Coventry Street School. At St George's Infant School the first of these meals was served on 4 October 1943; the dinner consisted of boiled mutton with vegetables and jam tart. The teachers helped with supervision and waited at the tables.

It was the Stourport Boys' and the Harry Cheshire schools that suffered most disruption, as a result of bomb damage in air raids. A Stourport resident recalls: 'The school was closed for quite a while afterwards. We had to go to school in shifts for a time after that. Some of us went to a class in the Church on Lickhill Road, which is now the Kingdom Hall of the Jehovah's Witnesses, some went to the girls' school which was near where the Bewdley Road traffic lights are now, and others went to the Methodist Rooms in Parkes Passage.' The Harry Cheshire School in Kidderminster had been open for less than a year when the damage suffered in the air raid on 24 May 1941 caused it to close for three weeks while it was patched up. William Bradley moved from St John's School to this school in September 1941. He recalls that for a while pupils still only attended on a part-time basis: 'boys in the morning and girls in the afternoon for a week, and then they swapped round'.

These events would have brought the realism of war graphically to the area's schoolchildren. Although Hazel Fallon's school was not directly affected, she has a vivid memory of the effects of bombing. 'Our PE Mistress and Music Mistress were also ambulance drivers. One night, when Coventry was badly bombed, they were there all night. In the morning they returned all dirty and came directly to school. They assembled the pupils and told those who lived nearby to go home and collect something for the people who had lost their homes. The children filled the school stage with rations and clothes and these were taken straight back to Coventry by the two mistresses.'

Schools tried to instil a sense of pride into their children by getting them to take part in 'Dig for Victory' schemes, helping at local farms or cultivating spare ground near the school. The Harry Cheshire School had allotments for pupils to cultivate and Foley Park Infants' School had a vegetable plot near the headmaster's (Mr Rose) office.

Peter Carter was at Hartlebury Grammar School:

Sports afternoon was on Wednesday. We chose between playing sports or helping farmers. I and my mates helped on a farm, thinning beet. The farmer was Mr Groves on Hartlebury common. He used to keep two little horn cups in his barn and always gave us cider in them (my first alcoholic drink). We also worked on farms during school holidays. With John Buchanan, who lived in Stanklyn Lane, I went to a farm at Hartlebury where we did fruit, pea and bean picking. We were paid 6d a pot (40lb of peas). On one occasion the farmer took the peas to market and for some reason he couldn't sell them so he brought them back; he sold me a pot for 6d! We also had allotments in the headmaster's huge garden. We each had a plot about 12ft by 12ft where we grew lettuce, etc. We were helping the war effort; 'digging for victory'.

It was a similar story for the girls at the high school says Margaret Phelan: 'We had parties who went out on sports afternoons. Instead of playing sport we went to nearby farms, sugar beet singling (thinning), potato picking or fruit picking. We camped for a fortnight out at a farm at Crowle picking plums when they were in high season. We were just given an empty sack to fill with straw and that was what we slept on; eight of us, in a bell tent. Great fun!'

Ann Mole also helped on the farms:

Once I went plum picking from school. We were told we could eat as many plums as we wanted – but after the first day we couldn't stomach any more. We were also told we would be paid for what we picked. I don't remember what we were paid – but I do remember that I didn't get a penny of it. When we got back to school it was "suggested" by the Head that the school needed a new bench seat and the money should be used for that. We had no say in the matter! The farm work was generally OK – but once I had to clean a drain out; I've never cleaned a drain since without thinking about that. It smelled dreadfully.

Other children helped with the potato harvest.

All the land around our church was farmed by Mr Garbutt, from Heightington, and in the potato season a master at school used to ask for volunteers to pick potatoes. I would sign up for that and we would have a week off at a time. We could go from class – it wasn't a holiday like half-term is today. My mother gave me a bottle of cold tea to drink whilst I was working. Some Stourport boys had never had cold tea and they were so impressed they swapped their dandelion and burdock for it.

All schools were very much involved with the war. Kidderminster High School 'adopted' the warship MV *Rothley* and the children knitted and made clothes for the crew – especially gloves and balaclava helmets. The crew were very grateful and on occasions the captain and other members of the crew visited the school and gave talks about the war and life on the ship.

Another military association was with the French. Margaret Phelan remembers:

Apart from knitting, which everyone did for the forces, we were especially linked with the French. The Headmistress was very friendly with Mrs Beakbane and we were encouraged to write and adopt Free French sailors who were coming over to fight with General de Gaulle. Ribbesford House at Bewdley was the Free French Training Academy for officers. Many of us wrote to Free French sailors; I don't know what they made of our letters. It was rather funny at the time. My head was turned as a 14-year-old having a letter that began: '*Ma Douce Fleur des Anges*' – 'My Sweet Flower of Angels'. I never met him, which was probably a very good job!

But what was it like in a Kidderminster school in those days? Roger Baulk spent his first schooldays in St George's Infant School from 1942 until July 1944.

There were three teachers at the school: the kindly but elderly Mrs Griffiths took the reception year – Class 3; Miss Rawlings, the Headmistress, took Class 2; and Miss Lunn taught the elder children in Class 1. The building was late Victorian and had high ceilings; the long deep windows had hoppers for ventilation operated by long cords with their ends wrapped around a hook on the wall. The heating was by heavy cast iron radiators with service pipes several inches thick. The playground had to be cleared for deliveries of coke to fuel the boilers. The toilets were spartan. One did not linger too long as they were outside at the bottom of the playground. Crossing the icy tarmac in winter was hazardous and water pipes and closets regularly froze

The building that was St George's Infant School, Leswell Street, April 2005. The foundation stone, hidden behind the wall, was laid on 19 July 1899. *(Bob Millward)*

up. In some parts of the school there were still overhead gas lights operated by on/off bars attached to chains.

School dinners came in steel containers from the canteen in Coventry Street. The cabbage was watery and the pastry was hard and flew off the plate when pressed hard with a spoon. However, we had to be grateful: we had food. Milk was delivered in tall metal churns and dispensed with metal ladles into our white, blue-rimmed enamelled mugs. In winter the milk was often frozen and in summer warm and sour.

Lessons were basic and restricted by the availability of materials. In Class 3 the ABC was shown on cards around the wall, and numbers were displayed on cards with coloured dots. Special 'laced up' cards were used to teach us how to tie shoelaces. We had slates and chalk for individual work. Later, numerical tables were learned by reciting them frequently. Boys learned to knit scarves and dishcloths and we regularly spent hours shredding material for stuffing toys.

The percussion band practices were enjoyed with flip charts showing each instrument's notes in different colours. Why was I the only boy in the cymbals group when there was just one girl in the drum section? There were also castanets, tambourines, primitive xylophones and, of course, the triangle. The year's highlight was the annual performance at the Town Hall attended by all parents and grandparents who could get there.

Physical exercise was team games in the playground, with coloured bands worn diagonally over one shoulder.

Clearly these activities would have been broadly similar, war or no war. Much of school life went on as normal. Christmas parties were still organised and Empire Day celebrated on or near 24 May. The children were taken to St George's Church for services on Ash Wednesday and Ascension Day; and to take Harvest Festival offerings. Attendances were, as usual, poor when there were epidemics of measles, chickenpox, mumps or, more seriously, scarlet fever. Inoculations against diphtheria continued to be administered. There was now, however, another church visit: that for the National Day of Prayer on 3 September – the date on which war was declared by Neville Chamberlain.

And when the war was over in 1945 the children were entertained, at a price, by an American woman. The St George's Infant School logbook records: 'Sept 25: Mrs Coatson, a Negro woman, entertained the children for thirty minutes this afternoon. She sang Negro spirituals and danced for them. She also told them a Negro slave's story. No recreation period was permitted in consequence; the normal timetable being resumed afterwards.'

There were rather different memories in some schools. 'Materials were very short,' said Graham Dowe. 'At King Charles paper was so scarce that we had to write on the covers of our exercise books and then turn them upside down to try and use every space. To get a new exercise book you had to go to the headmaster with the old one and he would tear the corner off – so it couldn't be used to claim another one.'

'I can remember the Nit Lady,' said his wife, June. 'She came regularly and looked into your hair – everybody was included. Those found with nits had to have their hair cut very short and it was, I suppose, a bit of a stigma; even those who normally had a short hairstyle were accused of having nits. I was at the New Meeting School and I remember being taken to the back of the church where there were piles of sandbags. We were told that we should go there if we were being bombed.'

Ann Mole knew the Nit Lady. 'The nurse who came round to check our health at school was also the Nit Lady. She married the pram shop man from Mill Street (Mr Price). If you had your hair in a bun, which was the fashion then, she would make you unroll it so she could check inside the roll.'

It was no doubt similar at Areley Common School. Roy Bayliss recalls:

We had medical inspections at school and were regularly visited by the Nit Lady, and the dentist who frightened you to death in his barbaric way. The school inspector, Mr Cooper, was also a frequent visitor. He would check which children hadn't been to school and would go round and see their parents. It was a very serious matter. If the parents couldn't provide a satisfactory reason for their absence, the children would get the cane when they came back to school; and if they were persistent offenders the police would get involved and the parents taken to court. We were frightened to death of Mr Cooper – even if we'd done nothing wrong.

It is fitting to end this chapter on a positive note. The school logbooks show that the human side of the education establishment did not disappear in those uncertain times. Despite the difficulties imposed on schools, it was not unusual for a teacher to be allowed seven to ten days away from school when husbands came home on leave.

9
LEISURE AND ENTERTAINMENT

Much has been made of the British character in the Second World War and the way that people were determined to keep up their spirits and make the best of things. There was no better example of this than the way in which people used their leisure time to take their minds off the many problems of the war – despite the austerity of wartime conditions. They did this in many ways: holidays, music, shows, theatre, dancing, films, concerts, sports, gardening and even just reading, walking or listening to the wireless.

Holidays were not as easily available as in pre-war times; troops and officials were given priority for transport; non-essential travel was discouraged and few private cars were in use because of petrol rationing. Beaches in the southern and eastern coastal resorts were cordoned off and much of the available accommodation was taken over by the military.

Nevertheless, some intrepid travellers did manage to arrange seaside holidays in coastal regions. Margaret Phelan with her mother and aunt enjoyed a break in Weston-super-Mare sometime in 1942. 'We left Kidderminster station at 8 a.m. The train was continually diverted into sidings to allow ammunition and troop trains through. It was 6.30 p.m. when we arrived at the station at Weston. There were no taxis, of course, so we walked and paid 6*d* to a boy to carry the luggage on a home-made cart. We stayed in a boarding house in Lower Church Road. Much bomb damage could be seen.'

Maurice Fallon remembers: 'Travel was difficult because of the restrictions and permission was often necessary – although people of sufficient means could manage to find ways. My sister became ill and we had to get a doctor's note to enable her to go by train to Llandudno to recuperate. She said that the town was full of soldiers and she rather enjoyed her time there watching them drilling on the sea front.'

When people did manage to get away it often wasn't far. 'In the war my dad had ten days' holiday and we had one day out. This was the annual visit to Malvern,' said Mike Compton. 'We took the bus to Worcester and then Malvern, walked up the hill to the café and then back down to catch the bus home. The buses had wooden seats and they weren't very comfortable. That was our holiday.'

The government actively discouraged travel in order to preserve the country's fuel resources for essential war activities. Posters advertised: 'Is your journey really necessary?' In 1942 the idea of 'Holidays at Home' was introduced, to encourage people to take a break, but remain in their own locality.

Kidderminster took to this idea and Holidays at Home events were organised over a three-week period from 25 July to 15 August. Most of the events were in Brinton and St George's parks: they included a bowls competition, shows, bands, dancing and many other activities. A swimming gala was held in the Baths and the Home Guard held a gymkhana at the Carpet Trades Sports Ground (White Wickets). The latter included performances by the Kidderminster Military Prize Band, a dancing troupe, a concert party, a conjuror/ventriloquist, Alf Tabb the Trick Cyclist, light refreshments and *ice cream*! For the competitive there was a variety of 'athletic' events.

Holidays at Home were staged again in 1943, and by 1944 the programme had expanded to last for four weeks.

The *Shuttle* edition for 5 August 1944 reports: 'Kidderminster has been very fortunate in its Holidays-at-Home arrangements. The committee have worked with such zest that the programme, which has been arranged to extend over four weeks, is not only of a very fine quality but also succeeds in providing for everybody – young and old alike.'

The opening ceremony had been on Saturday 29 July and 'all functions have been well patronised by patriotic folk, who have faithfully followed the Government's appeal to avoid travel'.

It was claimed that 'every minute of the day from 3 p.m. until blackout, there will be something going on in St George's and Brinton Parks'. In the first few days visitors to Brinton Park were regaled by a concert party from Worcester, the Revo Works Band from Tipton, Miss Dorothy Pugh's Dancing Troupe accompanied by the Blue Star Band and the Ventriloquist Professor Whyley. There was Dancing on the Green to music by George Whitford from 9 p.m. until blackout. Professor Duranti's Punch and Judy show attracted many grown-ups as well as children. On Tuesday night the RAPCATS played to an audience in excess of 3,000. Holidaymakers at St George's Park saw many of the above acts and were also treated to Ankle and Beauty competitions – won by Mrs Chadburn and Mrs Queenie Salter, respectively. Arthur Howley's Concert Party provided cheery fare including topical songs: *The Victory Polka*, *Maizy Doates* and *Tea for Two*.

Margaret Phelan sold raffle tickets to help fund the entertainments:

A stage was erected for the Concert Parties in St George's Park at the side of the bowling green – that very sacrosanct green lovingly tended by the elderly French gardener, Mr Le Loup, who lived opposite the park in Radford Avenue. He was very fierce to anyone not respecting his gardens and lawns. Patsie Heath's and Elsie Dyer's dancing classes gave shows, and sometimes you'd get bands performing: Fred Reynolds was playing at that time. I got roped in to sell raffle tickets in St George's Park on almost every night during the Holidays at Home period in August. Also involved were Robin Cooke, Hugh Kelly and Trevor Roden from the CMC carpet family. We had great fun seeing who could sell the most raffle tickets. We made our fun in those days; there wasn't much else.

Two of the many performing groups playing prominent roles in Holidays at Home events were the Rae Sneader Concert Party and the RAPCATS. Patti Silk remembers:

Mrs Rae Sneader had a hairdressing and beauty salon in Oxford Street, next door to her husband's jewellery shop. She had been a professional singer, and formed the Concert Party with Miss Fay Viner (Principal of the Dance and Elocution Studio), who did the choreography. We gave concerts in the Town Hall, Wolverley Hospital and many areas around the Wyre Forest; some were open-air concerts in the parks. The largest most spectacular event was the Anglo-American Show in the Town Hall. Guest stars from New York and Hollywood took part. No doubt they were in town because of the local US military hospitals. I was the principal dancer and partnered the star of the show, Billy Taft – who had been Betty Grable's partner on Broadway in *Dubarry was a Lady*. A drummer from the famous Tommy Dorsey Orchestra took part. This was Kidderminster's first live glimpse of Hollywood glamour.

We had our problems: materials for shows were not easily obtainable, and lengths of parachute silk and the softer silver barrage balloon fabrics were made use of. Our concert party raised over £20,000 for war effort charities at the same time

The

"R.
A.
P.
C.

REVUE

"*Holiday Express 1941*"

TOWN HALL

THURSDAY
FRIDAY · SATURDAY
JANUARY
23rd, 24th, 25th

★

BY KIND PERMISSION OF
LT.-COL. E. T. C. SMITH,
R.A.P.C.

A.
T.
S."

" Our true intent is all for your delight."—Shakespeare.

PROGRAMME

Front page of a RAPCATS programme at Kidderminster Town Hall, January 1941. *(Betty and Fred Sutton)*

A group of RAPCATS practising outside on a sunny day. Top to bottom: Joan Phipps, Jackie Bowen, Dink Eldridge and Betty Sutton. *(Joan Phipps)*

as providing much cheer for Kidderminster people in those austere war years.

The RAPCATS was a band and concert party taking its name from the Royal Army Pay Corps and the Auxiliary Territorial Service. 'It was an outlet for our energies and provided ourselves, and the people of Kidderminster, with some pleasure,' said Joan Phipps, who came to town as a member of the Pay Corps. 'We were very skilful – there were six or seven people in the band and quite a lot of others who did various acts. We tap danced, sang, did sketches and played music, travelling by military lorry to village halls near Kidderminster and other places.'

Fred and Betty Sutton, now living in Surrey, were enthusiastic members of the RAPCATS and enjoyed their time in town so much that they help to organise regular nostalgic weekend reunions. Fred recalled:

In those days there wasn't much other entertainment and our shows were very popular. We started in our NAAFI (Pike Mills garage) giving shows for fellow servicemen. They began to bring their landladies and people they were billeted with; gradually our reputation spread.

As we got more ambitious, some of our women soldiers went for lessons at the Dance and Elocution Studio over Woolworths. We developed quickly and put on some very impressive shows. One featured men with blackened faces, and it was said that the famous Black and White Minstrels were inspired by the Kidderminster RAPCATS shows.

We performed in the Town Hall, and sometimes the shows would be on for a week including a Saturday matinée. We also did outdoor performances in the local parks for the Holidays at Home scheme.

I particularly remember the trips to towns and villages around Kidderminster. On one occasion we were at a village hall that had no electricity and we had to use gas to light the stage; during rehearsals the piano kept rolling down the stage because the floor sloped. I asked a soldier to fix it and he knocked six-inch nails through the piano into the floor! We went to the local US camps and once played with Bob Hope. Any money we made went to wartime charities – particularly the Spitfire Fund.

I like to think that our activities became an integral part of life in Kidderminster. I was the pianist and would sometimes play in local pubs. People were so pleased to hear live music that I never had to buy myself a drink.

Betty Sutton added: 'In 1986 the Mayor and Mayoress came to our reunion and started a civic relationship which continued for many years. When the RAPCATS had their fiftieth anniversary the flowerbeds in Brinton Park were set out in the pattern and colours of the Pay Corps badge. The town has had two civic receptions for us and on the wall of the Town Hall is a plaque dedicated to the RAPCATS. We feel that we did so much that, if we hadn't been here, the town would have been much poorer socially.'

The local dance troupes run by Patsie Heath, Dorothy Pugh and Elsie Dyer contributed greatly to the entertainment scene. 'I was in the Patsie Heath dance troupe,' said June Dowe, 'but I also sang. We appeared on the bandstand in Brinton Park and in St George's Park on the circular mounds. The concerts were really well supported.'

Janet Holland as the Lopear Rabbit's assistant in the pantomime of *Babes in the Wood*, held in Kidderminster Town Hall in February 1942. (*Janet Cowburn*)

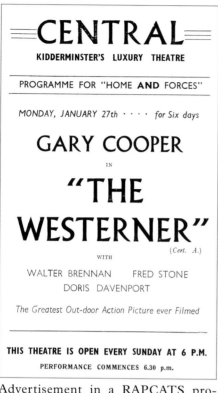

=CENTRAL=

KIDDERMINSTER'S LUXURY THEATRE

PROGRAMME FOR "HOME **AND** FORCES"

MONDAY, JANUARY 27th · · · · for Six days

GARY COOPER

IN

"THE WESTERNER"

(Cert. A.)

WITH

WALTER BRENNAN   FRED STONE

DORIS DAVENPORT

The Greatest Out-door Action Picture ever Filmed

THIS THEATRE IS OPEN EVERY SUNDAY AT 6 P.M.

PERFORMANCE COMMENCES 6.30 p.m.

Advertisement in a RAPCATS programme for a screening of *The Westerner* at the Central Cinema in Oxford Street, January 1941. *(Betty and Fred Sutton)*

'Two hours of bright and attractive entertainment, in these times of stress and worry, are provided by the pantomime *Babes in the Wood*, which is being presented by Rae Sneader and Patsie Heath at the Town Hall . . .' proclaimed a *Kidderminster Shuttle* review in February 1942. A large cast of local talent was listed in the 3*d* programme.

Janet Cowburn (née Holland) was the Lopear Rabbit's assistant and provides personal memories of the show:

We rehearsed for the show at Rushmore Studios above shops and offices in the High Street and in between gave cabarets at places like RAF Hartlebury, and Saturday night dances at the Florence Ballroom and the Black Horse. Gertie Westwood played the piano and Patsie Heath organised every minute of the practice sessions.

The show was packed out for every performance. In one of my acrobatic solos I wore an elasticated swimsuit onto which my mother had sewn thousands of sequins. When Rae Sneader sang she cupped cards in each hand on which she had written the words. On one occasion she was singing one of her serious songs when the audience started to titter, quietly at first and then louder. She stopped and asked them what was wrong. Her dress was tucked up in the back of her knickers. When she realised she turned back to the audience and said with a smile: 'Why didn't you tell me?'

Apart from organised activities, people made their own entertainment. 'Summertime swimming in the Severn at Stourport was popular, as was skating at Catchems End in the bad winter of 1940,' recalls one Kidderminster resident.

Others enjoyed walks or the cinema: 'There were some good walks at Spennells before the houses were built, and I often walked there with my husband-to-be who I had met at the Church Boys and Girls Brigade. We also went to the pictures if we could afford it. There were four cinemas in Kidderminster then: the Central, the Futurist, the Grand and the Empire (the latter two often referred to as 'fleapits'). It was 3*d* to go to the Empire and 9*d*, I think, to go into the front seats of the Futurist and the Central; more on the balcony – about 1*s* 9*d*.'

American films were popular and in January 1941 the Central was proud to screen *The Westerner* with Gary Cooper, billed as 'The greatest outdoor action picture ever filmed'.

There was much to choose from at the cinema. In the first week of August 1941 in Kidderminster there was *Tarzan's Secret Treasure* with Johnny Weissmuller and Maureen O'Sullivan at the Central; *Weekend in Havana* with Carmen Miranda, Cesar Romero, Alice Faye and John Payne at the Futurist; and the Grand was showing *Hot Spot* featuring Betty Grable, Victor Mature and Carol Landers. At the same time in Stourport the Haven screened *It's in the Air*, starring George Formby, for three days. The Garden Cinema in Bewdley boasted 'Every day a complete change of programme', including Stan Laurel and Oliver Hardy in *Saps at Sea*.

Bill Bury's diary reveals some of the films that he saw in 1941: Will Hay in *Ghost of St Michaels* at the Central, Bill Boyd in *Doomed Caravan* at the Grand and *Men of Boys Town* with Spencer Tracy at the Futurist. Other delights for this

One of Patsie Heath's dance troupes rehearsing for *Babes in the Wood*. Second from left: Miss Earp; third left: Janet Holland; fifth left: Margaret Rooke. (*Janet Cowburn*)

12-year-old in 1941 were: Pat Collins's Fair arriving on 13 June, Robert Fosset's Circus in September and George Sanger's Circus in April of the following year.

Marjorie Rivers used to travel from Shatterford into Kidderminster to the cinema. 'I often went to the Futurist in Vicar Street. It usually had my choice of film and it was handy – right by the bus stop. The Futurist had a lovely entrance – all red; and there were red upholstered seats.'

A trip to the cinema was special for Melvyn Thompson: 'It was a rare treat to go to the pictures. *Just William* seemed to have much in common with my gang, and George Formby and the Marx Brothers were very popular. But the real treat was a Saturday night walk to the Empire in the Horsefair for a seat in the sixpennies to see Hopalong Cassidy, Roy Rogers or the serial *Flash Gordon*.'

This was much more sophisticated than in some outlying villages. Roy Bayliss remembers:

> Entertainment in the village was very much up to ourselves. Mr Dilworth Lloyd and his sister had been missionaries and put on magic lantern shows in the parish rooms – possibly four times a year. They had a beautiful brass projector and showed slides taken abroad of missionary work, pictures of African people and places they had visited. She stood by the screen with a pointer whilst he worked the projector. We had dances in the parish rooms and occasionally the odd play or two. The women of the village had nights when they gathered to knit for the forces. Reg Wilcox's brother was in the navy and he once received socks knitted by the ladies of Areley Kings.

Dancing featured significantly in people's lives and ladies would no doubt enjoy the social activity after long shifts at work; the presence of so many US soldiers would have added something out of the ordinary. Jessie Maskell worked at Tomkinsons: 'We used to do day and night shifts. Of course, we made up for it when we were on days by going dancing every night. Ruth Watkins used to come with us sometimes: "Now stick together. No Yanks!" she used to say.'

There seemed to have been quite a few dance venues. Les Lench: 'There were plenty of dance halls: the Baths, the Gliderdrome (Florence ballroom), the Black Horse, the Fountain and there was also the Crown at Stourport. Big Bands came during wartime but I can't remember names. Fred Reynolds was the bandleader at the Florence.' Alf Mole used to escort his sisters to those same dance halls and also to The Lion and Frank Freeman's.

You didn't have to go out for entertainment. The BBC had, arguably, its finest period during the war and was ceaseless in its efforts to spread news and entertainment. Melvyn Thompson again: 'A typical evening was spent sitting at home in front of the coal fire playing cards or one of the games outlined in the book *The Brighter Blackout*. Apart from an old wind-up gramophone the "wireless" was the only media entertainment available. A favourite was Tommy Handley's *ITMA* programme, but my dad was a big fan of comedian Robb Wilton whose opening line was always: "The day war broke out my missus said to me . . ." On very special occasions I was allowed to sit up and listen to a boxing match.'

Reading was also widespread and there were alternatives to Kidderminster Library. 'We spent a lot of time indoors at night when I was a child,' said one gentleman. 'There was no encouragement to go out. My parents were members of Smith's Library so there was always something to read. I think I read more then, than I have done since.'

Lots of people had similarly modest ways of keeping themselves occupied in their leisure time. Melvyn Thompson recalls: 'When I was a boy I would spend the daylight hours with my friends across the golf links and around Spennells Pool and the stream that led from it towards Hoobrook. In those days the Pool had a tower with diving boards in the middle. We caught minnows and tadpoles or played football with a very old hand-sewn ball. On occasions my father would get a licence from Stanley Cattell's estate agents office in town and we fished in Captains Pool.'

GLIDERDROME Ball Room Kidderminster

DANCING

On the Finest Floor in the Midlands

M.C.: IVAN BARRIE, A.I.S.D.

(Late British School of Ballroom Dancing.)

EVERY MON., WED., FRIDAY & SATURDAY

	Admission H.M. Civilian Forces		Time p.m.
Mondays	1/3	1/0	7.30 to 11.30
Wednesdays	1/6	1/3	7.30 to 11.30
Fridays	2/0	1/6	8.00 to 12.00
Saturdays	2/6	1/6	8.00 to 12.00

CONTINUOUS DANCING

FULL GLIDERDROME BAND EACH EVENING

Musical Director: PHILIP COOPER

Vocalist: BERYL TURNER

Advertisement in the *Kidderminster Shuttle*, 11 August 1945, for dancing at the Gliderdrome, also known as the Florence. (*Kidderminster Shuttle*)

The churches with youth clubs and the uniformed organisations played a large part in keeping youngsters occupied. 'The Church Boys and Girls Brigade was very active,' remembers Eric Mole. 'We met regularly for all sorts of activities. A farmer let us keep a tent in his barn and some of us boys would go there camping at weekends. I got a lot of pleasure from that.'

Children in Lorne Street were lucky because the Baptist Church had a gym behind the church, with sprung floor, horizontal and parallel bars, vaulting boxes, fixed horizontal ladders and loose rings. In bad weather the caretaker Mrs Arnold used to let them in to play. Because it was a church they had a small heating allowance and a small coke fire to take the chill off. 'We played in there for hours,' says Alf Mole. 'Nearly every night of the week there was something going on for young people.' The government encouraged youth clubs to help children whose parents were both employed; father away in the army and mother working – perhaps nights. So youth clubs opened two or three times a week. George Street Methodist Church had a very lively club held in the big basement underneath the church, according to Margaret Phelan:

> It was a thoroughly enjoyable youth club. A lot of children from the High School and local Grammar Schools attended. We had debates, discussions, lively games and dancing. I gave the sermon at one youth club service in the church even though I wasn't a Methodist. It was a very worthwhile, very good club; I think we went about twice a week – during the blackout, too. In those days no one felt really nervous about a young girl going out at night. You might bump into a lamp-post and collect a few bruises but you never felt anything unpleasant would happen that you couldn't handle. There was also a council inspired youth club held in Foley Park Junior School, in Northumberland Avenue. We met in the big room and used smaller classrooms when splitting up for discussions, debates, meetings and other pastimes. This too was a most excellent club. I think its first leader was John Drake, the headmaster of the Grammar School; 'Johnny Drake' as people referred to him. I vividly remember he taught me how to quickstep. When he had set the club going on its feet, another headmaster, Harry Hodgkinson from New Meeting, took over as leader and he, too, encouraged some very good debates, classes in First Aid (essential in those days), gardening and other interesting things of the time.

Margaret Phelan is a member of the New Meeting Church and recalls 'that the hall to the side of the church was commandeered for use by the BBC Midland Light Orchestra – it all seemed rather top secret'.

Indeed, this orchestra had evacuated from their studio in Broad Street, Birmingham, to Kidderminster to avoid air raids. Bill Bury had personal experience of live broadcasts by the orchestra and shares those memories with us. As a young teenager in 1943 he was keen to learn to play the oboe and approached a member of the orchestra, who rented a house nearby, for advice. The upshot was a visit to the studio to meet Lucy Vincent, the oboist.

I was shown into the hall by the 'security man' and found myself in a room with no natural light – the windows having been sand bagged. Half the hall was formed into a stepped stage with approximately twenty-four chairs and music stands facing a conductor's rostrum. Microphones were suspended above. A console of switches could be seen through the window of the control room at the other end of the hall. A partition divided the canteen from the main hall. Musicians were relaxing: talking in groups or reading; a wind instrument 'tootled' in the background. Lucy Vincent chatted to me about my aspirations and after some brief instruction let me have a blow on her oboe. My first sounds were difficult to produce but I wasn't deterred. There was a call from the control room indicating the imminence of the broadcast and I was invited to stay (as long as I was quiet!).

Tuning up started with a cacophony of sounds and the announcer (Bernadette Hodgson, I think), complete with clipboard, took her place at a microphone. At another microphone stood Parry Jones, the celebrated Welsh tenor, and the conductor Rae Jenkins moved onto the rostrum. 'Stand by' was called, followed by a 'countdown'. At zero, a red light came on and the announcer said something like: 'This is the BBC Home Service.' I listened, enthralled, to my first experience of a live professional orchestra. I remember nothing of the programme except Parry Jones singing *Ombra Mai Fu* by Handel ('Largo'). The concert lasted for about forty-five minutes and consisted of marches, waltzes and selections from the shows: traditional fare for a Light Orchestra.

This was to be the first of three broadcasts that Bill was allowed to experience. He was hooked, and didn't miss any subsequent concert given by the orchestra in Kidderminster. Inevitably, he became an oboe player and still practises the art to this day.

Bill still has the programmes for the Town Hall Concerts given by the BBC Midland Light Orchestra, one of which is reproduced overleaf. This concert included such items as Offenbach's *Orpheus in the Underworld*, *Dance of the Hours* by Ponchielli, 'Ave Maria' by Schubert, sung by Mary Jarred, and Elgar's *Pomp and Circumstance* march No. 4. A notice on the programme read: 'In the event of an Air-Raid warning being received a notice will be displayed in the Auditorium. The concert will continue, but those wishing to leave may do so.'

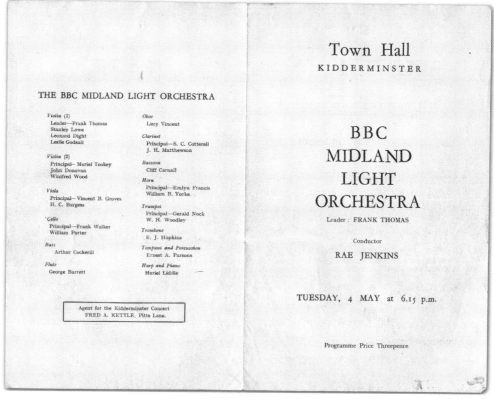

THE BBC MIDLAND LIGHT ORCHESTRA

Violin (1)
Leader—Frank Thomas
Stanley Lowe
Leonard Dight
Leslie Godsall

Violin (2)
Principal— Muriel Tookey
John Donovan
Winifred Wood

Viola
Principal— Vincent B. Groves
H. C. Burgess

'Cello
Principal—Frank Walker
William Porter

Bass
Arthur Cockerill

Flute
George Barrett

Oboe
Lucy Vincent

Clarinet
Principal—S. C. Cotterell
J. H. Matthewson

Bassoon
Cliff Carnall

Horn
Principal—Emlyn Francis
William B. Yorke

Trumpet
Principal—Gerald Nock
W. H. Woodley

Trombone
E. J. Hopkins

Timpani and Percussion
Ernest A. Parsons

Harp and Piano
Muriel Liddle

Agent for the Kidderminster Concert
FRED A. KETTLE, Pitts Lane.

Town Hall
KIDDERMINSTER

BBC
MIDLAND
LIGHT
ORCHESTRA

Leader : FRANK THOMAS

Conductor
RAE JENKINS

TUESDAY, 4 MAY at 6.15 p.m.

Programme Price Threepence

Programme cover for a concert given by the BBC Midland Light Orchestra at the Town Hall, Kidderminster, May 1943. *(Bill Bury)*

Many normal peacetime hobbies and activities continued, if in a truncated fashion. In 1942 the Dalley Rabbit Club held an Open Show in St John's Institute in August, and in the same year the local darts, bagatelle, bowls, football and cricket leagues were still operating. The Harriers matches had ceased for the War but Kidderminster Cricket Club beat Stourbridge by 5 wickets in the Birmingham League – captain Alec Wyers scoring 81 runs.

There was a wide variety of entertainment available during those war years, not necessarily over-elaborate or too highbrow. But it is easy to believe that with the constant threat of enemy bombing, shortages of most commodities, restrictions on movement and loved ones often fighting abroad that anything which contributed towards lifting the oppression of war was welcomed. It is a credit to the character of the local people, and to those who put themselves out to entertain them, that the local civilian population largely remained mentally unscarred by the war.

10

PULLING TOGETHER

Many strategies were adopted by individuals, groups and officialdom to cope with the stresses of life endured during the Second World War. We have discussed elsewhere the benefits of entertainment, the effect of food shortages, how locals related to the presence of military units, about co-operation in the workplace, involvement in air-raid precautions and the impact that evacuees from more dangerous abodes had on schools and the local population.

In this chapter we deal with some other ways in which people sustained themselves, their families, their town and the nation's war effort.

One important aspect of the co-operative effort was raising funds to enable the military machine to expand and function efficiently. Higher taxes were one means by which the government tackled this problem but there were others of a more personal, voluntary nature.

The War Office initiated a War Savings Campaign in November 1939 and Regional Savings Committees, originally set up during the First World War, were re-established. Alderman E.G. Eddy chaired the Kidderminster Savings Movement, which promoted investment in Saving Stamps, National Savings Certificates and War Bonds. Saving Stamps were a way of making small, regular contributions; when sufficient stamps had been collected, they could be converted into Certificates or Bonds.

It was not necessary to deal directly with the Post Office to take part in these financial schemes; patriotic inhabitants went round selling 6d National Savings Stamps door-to-door to neighbours. 'Lou Tolley's daughter Edna did this in Larches Road,' according to Monica Hill, and Robert Barber reports that 'Mrs Smith, a postmistress at the Lister Road post office, called regularly at houses in that area.'

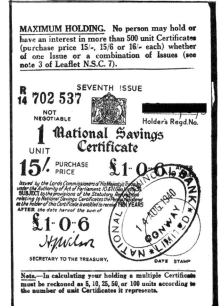

A wartime National Savings Certificate. (*Jeremy Thomas*)

Schools also encouraged children to buy savings stamps on a regular basis although an overenthusiastic and insensitive teacher could sometimes misjudge the situation. One High School girl who had won a scholarship to what, by local standards, was a somewhat exclusive school, was humiliated by her form teacher. 'I was made to stand up in class and asked why I hadn't brought Charity Money or bought National Savings Stamps. I was lectured with "Don't you realise there is a war on, girl?" Of course I knew there was a war on. My father was overseas in North Africa fighting it and it was all my mother could do to keep me in school uniform.' The problem was solved by her grandmother. She gave her a half-crown to buy the stamps. On the way home the stamps were cashed in so that there was money to buy them next week. Perhaps this was a case where 'pulling together' was not working in quite the way intended, but was an object lesson in how to deal with a difficult personal situation.

There was a better, less intimidating way of fostering a savings disposition: competition. In Worcestershire a silver Challenge Cup was awarded each month for the borough contributing the highest savings in proportion to its population in the previous month. In December 1940 Kidderminster, with a total savings of £155,440 yielding £4 17s 3d per head, came second to Dudley which averaged £6 13s 9d per head.

The *Kidderminster Shuttle*, shameless with patriotic jingoism in its attempts to spur locals to support National Savings, published this ditty on 7 December 1940 during 'War Weapons Week':

> War Weapons Song
>
> I'm going to sing a little song
> You've never heard before
> You won't find it a bore
> And this is what it's for;
> This week we've got to find some cash
> Our country to defend
> And as we buy our War Bonds
> We'll be singing as we lend:
>
> Chorus
> War Weapons week! War Weapons week!
> Come on get your money ready
> Hand it all to Mr Eddy.
> We'll kick old Hitler's pants, and punch
> Old Musso on the head
> If you only roll the money in
> For War Weapons Week

We recall that Mr Eddy was Chairman and Secretary of the Kidderminster Savings Movement.

But war savings were not just about stamps, certificates and bonds; special week-long events based on specific themes were organised to promote savings. Thus Kidderminster held campaigns for War Weapons Week, Warship Week, Tanks to Attack, Wings for Victory, Salute the Soldier and finally, in 1945, Thanksgiving Week. A plaque to commemorate the magnificent £584,994 raised for the Wings for Victory drive is in the entrance to the Town Hall.

These events were popularised by large military parades around the town, finishing up in Brinton Park. *Monica Hill saw most of those parades:*

There were Girl Guides, Boy Scouts, the Pay Corps, a contingent from each of the American camps at Burlish and Wolverley, detachments of the Home Guard, Civil Defence, the Fire Services; and civilian workers. But the highlight for us young females was the FREE FRENCH CADETS. Oh Boy! They were really smart; like toy soldiers. They had navy blue uniforms with floppy berets or the sort of caps that the Foreign Legion wore. They didn't wear greatcoats, they wore capes; and they were very romantic. The Americans beside them looked a shambles; ambling along chewing gum. These lads came behind them and didn't it show them up. Everybody turned out and clapped and cheered; it was quite a show.

Plaque on a wall in the entrance to Kidderminster Town Hall, Vicar Street, marking the award for high achievement in the Wings for Victory Appeal, 1943. *(Bob Millward)*

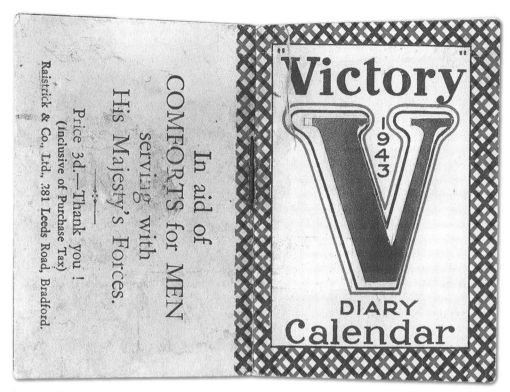

Cover of a simple diary sold to raise funds to provide 'Comforts for Servicemen'. *(Sally C. Brown)*

Mike Compton recalls fundraising for Spitfires:

> Towards the end of the war we had a propaganda exercise. A Messerschmitt 109, full of bullet holes, was parked in the fire station yard at Stourport. It had obviously been shot down. Presumably this was showing what Spitfires could achieve and what type of planes the enemy had. I actually went and sat in it.

Other sorts of fundraising took place at the same time. Simple diary calendars were sold to provide 'comforts for servicemen'. Inside was advice on recognising war gases.

But it was not just fundraising that was important; direct help and material support were also vital.

Thus in January 1941 an appeal for binoculars was advertised in the *Shuttle*. 'Every pair of binoculars is urgently needed. We are glad to learn that a number have already been brought in but it is estimated that there are many in Kidderminster who have these precious "eyes" and could render the country a distinct service by allowing the Government the use of them even if unwilling to dispose of them.'

Security was also an issue and posters warned that 'Careless talk cost lives', 'Your words are his weapons' and other similar counsel. Fundamental to security monitoring was the identity card, which had to be carried with you at all times.

Some families fixed a large map to the living room wall and took comfort by sticking in pins to trace what they thought might be the route taken by a loved one fighting overseas. Places mentioned on news bulletins were a vital part of this cathartic process even if much of what they heard was imprecise.

Schools became involved directly in the support system. Sheila Kirk recalls girls' 'sewing' lessons at St George's School. 'This consisted of unravelling pieces of cloth into individual threads. These were put into sacks and I assume sent off to be re-spun. It was called our War Effort. And we knitted kettle holders for soldiers – what on earth for?'

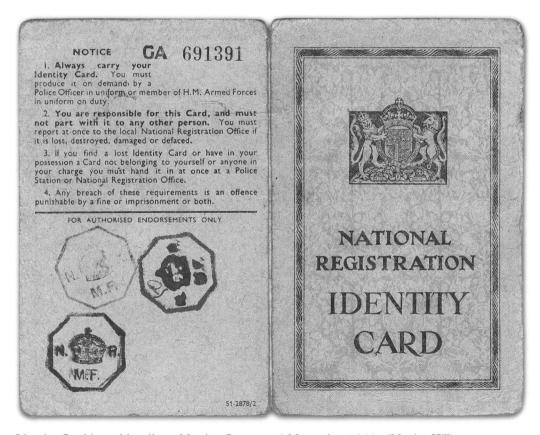

Identity Card issued locally to Monica Carter on 3 November 1944. *(Monica Hill)*

Families looked out for each other in many ways. In the annual Kidderminster Allotment Competitions George Millward won first prize on the Aggborough site in 1945 despite being away from home with the RAF. In fact, it was his father who deserved the award; he had been maintaining George's patch as well as his own.

The WVS was tremendously important in providing succour in all sorts of ways. Monica Hill recalls:

> They started a Rest Centre in the Mill Street Wesleyan Methodist Church. When people were bombed out in Birmingham they were brought down by coach and given soup, blankets and camp beds until they could be found somewhere to stay.

Nell Carter was a WVS volunteer when she heard of a scheme initiated by cigarette companies who offered to send parcels of 200 cigarettes to any local servicemen serving overseas – at cost price. She was determined that they should all have these cigarettes, so raffles, whist drives, bring-and-buy sales and so forth were organised; an advert was placed in the *Shuttle* asking for names and addresses. She got enough for all, but her favourites were the 7th Worcesters (the Local Territorials from the Shrubbery) because by then they had been sent to Burma. After a few months there came a flow of service air-letters from Burma: 'Thank you' and 'God bless you', 'We thought we were forgotten'.

It was perhaps the men and women serving and fighting abroad who needed their spirits bolstering from 'back home'. Many groups and institutions, as well as individuals, sent parcels of food and toiletries to make life a little easier; and of course the *Shuttle* or *Times* would keep them up to date with what was happening.

Nevertheless, for most service people it would be family communication, both ways, that would be uppermost in their priorities; and the only viable way of doing this then was by letter. It is a moot point as to whether Arthur Williams's letter home would have comforted his family or merely alerted them to the dangerous situations that he could find himself in. Arthur was writing from somewhere in Europe on 14 February 1945 and was concerned that he hadn't received mail or a parcel since his 'Christmas treat'. He goes on to describe events that must have been on his mind since December 1944:

> I can now tell you of my first meeting with the Boche. We were roused from our beds one morning with the warning that we were being attacked. I was with four others in a mud-walled building. I lay in the doorway watching down the alleyway onto a road. We were there for about an hour and nothing happened

apart from the din from Jerry's mortar. All seemed to go quiet and the Sgt. in charge came and told us all was well and that he thought Jerry was withdrawing. We waited wondering what was happening and could hear spasmodic firing well away from us, when suddenly, a voice called out to us to hold our fire. It turned out to be a Cpl from another company who told us to lay down our arms and come out with our hands up; the whole village was surrounded. There was your hubby a POW and hadn't ever seen a Jerry. Soon we saw guns pointed at us from all directions.

They put us in a house but never attempted to search us. When we asked if we could smoke they gave their consent; we all expected that when we took the cigarettes from our pockets we should lose them, but no, they only took one after persuasion. I still had the cigars the kiddies sent me for Xmas and I got through the lot and dozens of cigs besides. We all smoked like chimneys thinking if they didn't have them, some of their other countrymen would. Soon more of our chaps were brought in, in fact, all

Pte Arthur Williams 'D' Coy, 1st Battalion Glasgow Highlanders, from Dudley Street, Kidderminster. *(Graham Williams)*

my own section and the rest who were in the house with us. We went to our billets to get hold of some of our gear. I wanted to get the remains of my parcel: cake, biscuits, cigarettes and a letter I had nearly completed for you. I was out of luck, couldn't find any trace of it. They made no attempt to take away any of our rations.

They took us into a farm building for our own safety, so it seemed, as our own chaps started sending over a few eggs. In the end they marched us off into the open country and put us all in a long ditch. We have to thank someone for moving us from the farm buildings as one of our tanks simply blasted the whole place. It was hell in that ditch, shelled, mortared and machine-gunned by both our own chaps and Jerry. When our guards heard tanks they jumped for joy, 'Panzers, Panzers' they cried. What a shock when they saw a Sherman tank. And that was that for them, they just changed places with us and we were free again after eight hours of Jerry hospitality.

Arthur stopped writing there, and when he began again he had received two letters from his wife and one from his parents.

'I won't re-write all this when writing to Dad & Mum, you can tell them; it'll save me writing time and also the censors. I was completely behind the times about Graham starting school and that he didn't like the idea. Thanks for the paper & envelopes, I'll write again as soon as I can.'

Family matters, the need to reassure and seek reassurance, humour, concern, cigarettes and rations permeate this moving letter.

Clarice Millward, whose father was killed in the First World War, would have needed something to maintain her morale when her husband George enlisted with the RAF in May 1941.

Support came from family members but mail home from George was important too, and no doubt she was reassured that he was suitably fed in Italy on Christmas Day 1944.

Letters from overseas came in typically flimsy Air Mail envelopes and those from sensitive areas were subject to censorship – usually by an officer. Writers could endorse the letters saying that the letter only contained family matters but there was no guarantee that they would not be opened anyway and checked for anything which would be helpful to the enemy.

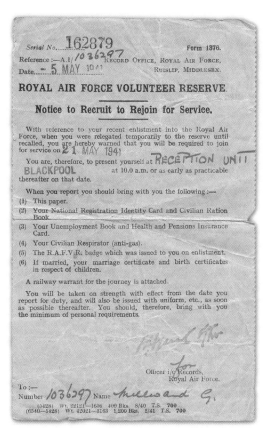

RAF enlistment document for George Millward. *(Phill Millward)*

Christmas menu for RAF 6 Squadron in Italy, 1944. *(Phill Millward)*

Typical Air Mail letter sent home by a serviceman. Note the censor's stamp. *(Jeremy Thomas)*

There was an even more formal wording pre-printed on certain service envelopes stating: 'I certify on my honour that the contents of this envelope refer to nothing but private and family matters.' But even signing to that was no bar to them being scrutinised. It must have been embarrassing for a soldier to know that someone other than the person the letter was intended for would be reading it.

The overwhelming sentiment conveyed to us by the many contributors to this book is that the people of the Kidderminster area found that the best way to get through those dreadful years of war was by co-operating with others in supporting the war effort – and each other. Their message was essentially 'We all pulled together.'

11

PEACE CELEBRATIONS

VE Day (Victory in Europe Day) was declared on Tuesday 8 May 1945. In the following weeks parties were held throughout the country in cities, towns and villages. Everyone celebrated the end of the threat from Nazi Germany.

Thousands flocked into London, making for Buckingham Palace to catch a glimpse of King George VI, the Royal Family and Winston Churchill.

Countless children's parties were organised on VE Day but perhaps the majority would have been arranged for the following day, allowing time to organise events. Children were able to sample some of the good things of which they had been deprived by rationing. Food would have been the main item to consider when planning the parties.

In Kidderminster, both sports fields at Aggborough and Hoo Road were packed with children on Tuesday afternoon and evening. Sumptuous teas were provided and the Mayor and Mayoress (Cllr and Mrs G.S. Chadwick) were present during the afternoon. Mrs Roberts, of 29 Oakhill Avenue, was the principal organiser. The evening's entertainment consisted of sports, games and a bonfire.

Thanksgiving services were held in churches, community halls and clubs. A service conducted by the Rev. W.L. Dicker was held at the Old Pals' shelter in Brinton Park on VE Day. On Wednesday the Old Pals were entertained by Mr W. Fisher of the Kidderminster Brewery and Mr Hardiman of Station Hill. On Thursday the Ray Brothers (bakers, of Wood Street) provided afternoon tea.

On Wednesday the main event in Stourport was a Victory parade from Memorial Park comprising British and US Army contingents, Police, Civil Defence Services, NFS, Boy Scouts, Girl Guides, Cadets and various other uniformed bodies. Upon returning to the park the UDC Chairman, Mr R.P. Vale, read an address from the Home Secretary, Herbert Morrison. Dancing outside the Swan Hotel went on until midnight, and a large bonfire on Stagborough Hill could be seen for miles around. The NFS made a blaze of old incendiary bombs in the fire station yard at New Street. (Presumably, they knew what they were doing!)

According to the *Shuttle* report, High Street and Worcester Street in Kidderminster were decorated, and throughout the rejoicings the behaviour of the crowds was most orderly. Other notable decorations in the town were: a carpet in Carpet Trades' show window in Mill Street bearing the full face of

Winston Churchill complete with cigar; and, on top of the gas holder, a large Union Jack and streamers fluttering high above the town.

More street parties were held when VJ Day (Victory over Japan Day) was celebrated on Wednesday 15 August 1945; some places would have had two parties within a few months. The Prime Minister, Clement Attlee, had announced the news at midnight when most people were in bed but church bells were not rung; little was known generally until the news bulletin at 8 a.m. on Wednesday morning.

The two-day VJ celebrations in Kidderminster followed a similar pattern to those adopted for VE Day. The tower of the Parish Church was floodlit on Wednesday evening and many went to admire the illuminations. A thanksgiving service was held at 11 p.m. in the church; Mayor Cllr G.S. Chadwick was in attendance. Perambulators with sleeping babies filled the entrance of the nave, while uniformed British, American and Allied soldiers, sailors and airmen joined the congregation, which included people from most parts and churches of Kidderminster. On one side of the chancel arch hung the American Stars and Stripes flag, and on the other hung the Union Jack with the colours of the 7th Battalion of the Worcestershire Regiment.

One reporter felt that no great effort had been made officially to mark the event as a 'Red Letter Day' to live forever in the memory; little was organised of outstanding merit commensurate with the greatness of the occasion. Streets were decorated with flags and bunting, and bonfires were lit at many locations with a huge bonfire and firework display in Brinton Park. On Sunday 19 August a thanksgiving service was held in the park followed by a victory march-past consisting of British and Empire forces and Civil Defence workers. While all these events brought a measure of enjoyment, the *Shuttle* reporter was of the opinion that greater pleasure was experienced at the many private and semi-private parties – and that was probably the case.

If going to parties wasn't your 'cup of tea' you could have treated yourself to a night at the Central Cinema in Oxford Street; screening from Monday 13 August for six days was *Great Day* starring Eric Portman and Flora Robson. Alternatively, the Gliderdrome Ball Room in Blackwell Street was open every Monday, Wednesday, Friday and Saturday. The admission charge was 1*s* 3*d*, 1*s* 6*d*, 2*s* and 2*s* 6*d* respectively, with a reduction for servicemen. A full band was present each evening.

Quite predictably, people had very different reactions to the ending of hostilities; from sober reflection to exuberance: 'On VE day I went to St Mary's Church in the morning by myself.'

'On VJ night there were celebrations in the park and singing in the town; it was quite something.'

Here are further recollections of those heady times:

Youngsters in the Horsefair on VE Day used an old suit of clothes to make a dummy bearing a remarkable resemblance to Adolf Hitler, and paraded around the streets laughing and shouting. In the evening it was burned on a huge bonfire.

Maureen Lawrence and Peggy Guest attended a Victory party in Aggborough Crescent: 'Trestle tables were aligned along Malvern Drive.' Red jellies and pink blancmange remain fixed in their memories – not to mention the delicious deep yellow home-made ice cream. 'In the evening there was a bonfire on land near the sand quarries owned by Mr Whitehouse. There was a "guy" on top and Vic Summers lit the fire with matches someone had brought back from Germany.'

Mike Compton, of Abberley, recalls:

Towards the middle of 1945 people began to appreciate that the war was going to end soon. The first we heard was when a lady came to school and said that a German radio station had broadcast that the war was over. The Headmaster proclaimed a two-day holiday and we went home cheering. Afterwards, the infants' teacher came round and said that because there had been no official statement we had to go back to school the following day. However, it was announced officially later that night so we didn't have to go to school after all.

The next day there was to be a big wedding in Abberley village. The bride was marrying a high-ranking army officer who had been invalided out of the war. He went to the Manor Arms that night and bought beer for all the men of the village before his wedding the following day.

That was the only celebration in the village at that time – but at Christmas we had a big party with food, games and a firework display. Fireworks weren't generally available but an ex-Signaller had got hold of a large quantity of military rockets and bangers. They were very exciting; I'd never seen fireworks before. It was said that an old gentleman at Pensax was so frightened that he hid in the cellar thinking the war had started again.

Marjorie Rivers was teaching in Worcester during the war but lived in Shatterford at weekends. 'We celebrated VE and VJ days by dancing at Trimpley village hall. A lot of the locals preferred Trimpley to Arley: it was just as far to walk but didn't seem so. Arley people were, I don't know, not so jovial as Trimpley people. We used to cycle to the dances there and, on one dark night, I was going round the corner by Park Attwood Lodge when a bat flew into my hair. I remember that! It was as frightened as I was. We also had a bonfire on the green on Trimpley Road.'

Jackie Bayliss: 'We were all too poor around here to afford street parties –
although there were some in Stourport. I remember that the Choir and Youth
Club let off fireworks from the top of Areley Kings church tower. In the
afternoon everybody went to Stourport where crowds of people were dancing,
cheering and letting off fireworks.'

The *Shuttle* of 18 August 1945 reported the disappearance of the police
traffic pulpit in Kidderminster:

> Cars driving through the town at midnight on the evening of the VJ
> celebrations were surprised to find a British Tommy stood in the wooden
> police pulpit at the bottom of High Street decked in a top hat directing the
> traffic with a party of local belles dancing round his feet.
>
> On Thursday morning passers by, observing a heap of ashes where the
> stately green pulpit once stood, lamented the passing of Kidderminster's
> unique landmark, little knowing that this treasured possession had been
> tactfully withdrawn in a rather battered condition to Pitts Lane before the
> revellers could express themselves in forms of fire.

Margaret Phelan relays her somewhat different version of this event:

> I don't remember much about VE night, only that it was rather damp and wet.
> But VJ night was different; it was mild. I went to my friend's in Larches Road,
> and her father had rigged up bird-scarers around his trees to go bang at
> intervals. I came away with another friend towards midnight. When we got to
> the Bull Ring there were a couple of soldiers, a sailor and I think an American
> or two, setting fire to paper and trying to burn the wooden pulpit. They weren't
> successful. We backed into the recess of Attwoods' windows and watched.
> They knocked the pulpit over and rolled it like a giant rolling pin through the
> Bull Ring into Trinity Lane and down to the river. We watched, a bit scared not
> knowing if we were going to be the next to be tossed in. They hoisted it over
> the railings and dumped it into the river. Ken Tomkinson's book, *Kidderminster
> Since 1800*, says that the police had removed it for fear of vandalism. But I am
> afraid that the police were a bit too late – it was already vandalised.

Vera Badger, resident of Lorne Street in 1945, recalls their street celebrations:

> No committee was set up; it was just generally decided to hold a party for
> Lorne Street residents. Food was scarce but everyone contributed from their
> rations. People tended to stock up for emergencies and I was in the habit of
> putting food items in a box in the cellar: a tin of salmon, a couple of jellies,
> something for a special occasion – and this was a special occasion. Unlike

s away from someone and not
one in their street. We looked
ed that we would give whatever
and home-made cakes. Some
eggs for baking; or there was
't taste so good but we were

but, for us, Milton Hall was
r musical chairs. The tea party
as just great to have something

Alf
Lo

mber VE and VJ day parties in
d firework display opposite the

Lorne Street/Villiers Street VE celebrations. The group in front of the Milton Hall Baptist Church includes Pauline Alderson, Shirley Anderson, Mrs Arnold, Vera Badger, Bill Barker, Sheila Barker, Ann Clarke, Malcolm Cook, Mrs Dalton, Val Davis, Mrs Gladman, Mrs Gorfankl, Mrs Harrison, Mrs Hopkins, Eunice Humphries, Joan Humphries, Mrs Humphries (1), Mrs Humphries (2), Mrs Humphries (3), Gerald Jay, Jean Jay, Arnold Kirkland, Patsy Maiden, Heather Mandon, Pamela Manners, Wendy Manners. Guy Massey, Alf Mole, Flo Mole, Madeleine Parke, Mrs Parker (1), Mrs Parker (2), Sheila Parker, Mrs Pearce, Mr Pearce, Sheila Pearsall, Sheila Pearson, Laurie Pritchard, Beatrice Rathbone, Geoff Rathbone, Allan Robinson, Mrs Routley, Muriel Routley, Revd T.J. Rowland, David Smith, Mrs Smith, Diana Thompson, Mrs Thompson, Colin Weavers. *(Jill Jackson)*

Poplar Road VE celebrations. Included in the photograph are Gerald Addison, Margaret Barber, Robert Barber, Stella Barber, Dennis Bentley, Eric Bradley, Dulcie Brooks, Peter Brooks, Gerald Brothers, Gwen Brothers, Joan Brothers, Mrs Campbell, Robert Cole, John Collier, Miss Collier, Bill Connolly, Geoff Connolly, Joan Connolly, John Connolly, Maurice Connolly, Tony Connolly, Barbara Cowley, June Dalton, Mrs Darkes, Michael Dickinson, Miss Dickinson, Rose Eaton, Ronette Eaton, Geoffrey Edwards, Ken Fido, Kenneth Franklin, John Hooper, John Mayall, Sheila Newell, Mrs Smith, Shirley Smith, Terry Smith, Shirley Summers, Charles Thacker, Pat Wagstaff, Raymond Williams. *(Robert Barber)*

Baptist Church. It singed the paintwork on the doors of nearby garages and melted a hole in the road right through the tarmac. We had army thunder flashes – and very loud they were, too.'

Members of the Poplar Road Beetle Club organised a victory party on Thursday 10 May. It is likely that Mrs Smith, seen dressed as Britannia on the right of the photograph above, and Rose Eaton (front, far left) were two of the main organisers. More than sixty children attended the party and after a splendid tea were given donkey rides. Poplar Road was a friendly neighbourhood, and most knew each other's names from one end of the road to the other – and beyond. Everyone provided what they could and all had a good time. The highlight of the day was when every child was given an orange, a bag of sweets, ice cream and a *3d* bit. Mr Connolly donated the ice cream

Crane Street VJ party. Among those photographed are Bill Booton, Mrs Booton, Floss Bunn, Graham Bunn, Mrs Gladys Davis, John Davis, Pauline Davis, Mrs Greenow, Daisy and Patricia Harris, Mrs Johnson, Barry Onslow, Mrs Poole, Shirley Pritchard, Edith Pudner, Mr and Mrs Rogers, Mrs Yates, Bobby Young, Terence Young, Mrs Young. *(John Davis)*

and Mr Crisp the 3*d* pieces. On the photograph some are shown still with their oranges and sweets but others just couldn't resist the urge to try their rare treats. The evening finished with singing and dancing for the older people with Jack Barber and his wife Ruby giving some fine vocal renditions.

A few children in the photograph didn't actually live in Poplar Road but lived nearby or had relatives living in the road. The photograph was taken at the entrance to the allotments where eight years later the Coronation party for Queen Elizabeth II was to be held.

Mrs Greenow, Mrs Sewell, Mrs Bunn, Mrs Pudner and Mrs Morris met at Hilda Pritchard's house, 15 Crane Street, to help organise their street VJ festivities. Hilda Pritchard's husband, Bill, was a baker working at Woolley's in Hall Street before moving to Collins' shop on the Butts, so sandwiches and cakes would have been well catered for. However, the majority of folk would have provided food of one sort or another. This was collected in the yard of Daisy Harris, the funeral director's wife. There was lots of spare wood stacked in the yard left over from coffin-making, and this was taken to help build a bonfire in the road at the junction of Crane Street with Bennett Street. Coffin trestle tables were used for the party. It was a lovely sunny day with most people in dresses or shirtsleeves. John Davis's father, Alfred, took responsibility for looking after the fire. 'He was worried about the closeness of such a large fire to the houses; we would never get away with it today. There wasn't a party for VE Day.'

Mr and Mrs Silcox ran the general stores and grocery delivery business in Woodward Road and were responsible for organising a party for the combined Brinton Crescent and Woodward Road VE celebrations. 'Everyone lent a hand and food was prepared at many houses. There was no hall available but fortunately it was a sunny day and many were in shirtsleeves; nobody seemed to mind, it was just such a joyous occasion.'

It was reported in the *Shuttle* on 19 May 1945 that about fifty children celebrated VE Day with a tea party in Dudley Street. Mr W. Tipper accompanied by Mr H. Edwards provided musical entertainment. There were also donkey rides for the children; Mrs Hughes loaned the donkey and Mr G. Bullen acted as groom. Each child received a bag of sweets and an orange – these rare treats being donated by Mr Taylor and Mrs W. Tipper. £1 3s 6d was left over after the party and it was agreed to put this towards the VJ celebrations – whenever that was to be.

Woodward Road and Brinton Crescent VE Day celebration. Those pictured include Ray Culwick, Mrs James, Ray Quinn, Mrs Sewell, Mr Silcox, Mrs Silcox, Mervyn Silcox, Bob Smith, Mrs Smith, Gwen Stokes, Mrs Stokes, Mrs Webb, Peter Webb, Mrs Yarrington. *(Mervyn Silcox)*

A peace celebration party marking VE Day in Dudley Street. Raymond Williams (in the high chair) is being fed by Beryl Rann. *(Graham Williams)*

The *Shuttle* of 12 May 1945 praised some street decorations. 'Reference has already been made to street decorations, but one feels that a special word of praise is due for Wood Street and Dudley Street which were quite the best decorated thoroughfares. Flags and streamers hung right across the roads and the houses were a mass of flags and coloured bunting, most of which had been carefully preserved since the Coronation.'

Wood Street held VE celebrations on Saturday 12 May and the residents met for a party in a bunting-strewn street.

Three separate parties were arranged in Wood Street for the VJ celebrations – all at the same time. The party near The Sportsman public house was organised by Mrs Darkes, Mrs Whitfield, Mrs

A crowded VE Day street party in Wood Street. *(Geoff Jukes)*

VJ party group in Sutton Park Road, 16 August 1945. The group includes Jean Brooks, Mrs Busby, Pam Busby, Graham Dowe, June Dowe, Marguerite Dowe, Bess Downing, Mrs Downing, Evelyn Haddock, Bernard Hughes, Roy Hughes, Eric Jones, Pam Jones, Jessie Jones, Susan Jones, Edna Maiden, Sheila Maiden, Audrey Moule, Brian Moule, Alan Padgett, Mrs Rowe, Mr Rowe, Edith Watkinson, Eva Watkinson, Mary Watkinson, Dinah Wilcox, Patrick Wilcox, Pauline Wilcox, Peggy Williams, Mrs Williams, Mr Williams (the piano teacher saved by his grand piano during an air raid – see Chapter 3, 'Under Fire'). Behind them are the remains of the bomb crater shown in Chapter 3. *(Pam Melloy)*

Cooper and Mrs Brookes. Jean Howley and her friends gave an evening concert and there was dancing and fireworks in the floodlit street; the celebrations lasted until midnight. Chapel Street won the prize for the best decorations and Wood Street was awarded £1 10s as runner-up. The prize money, together with monies left over from the party, was reserved for a sports day at King Charles School to be held on 25 August; the entire street was invited.

Graham Edginton recalls that there were several Victory parties arranged in Sutton Park Road: 'There was a celebration bonfire held in a field owned by Mr and Mrs Beddoes close to Rifle Range Lane. It was there that I was introduced to a young lady, Muriel Hartland, who was attending with a work colleague. We were married in 1952 and have been together ever since.'

The inhabitants of some streets, such as Clarence Street and Leswell Street, joined together for their VE party celebrations (see page iv).

The *Kidderminster Shuttle* reported that returning prisoners of war were also welcomed home with parties. 'Celebrations were held at St John's Institute on

A festive group from Neville Avenue celebrating victory includes Mrs Allen, Mrs Bird, Angela Bradley, Mrs Bradley, Mrs Martin, Brian Pearsall, Charles Pearsall, Gladys Pearsall, Mr Randle, Mrs Randle, Lucy Randle, Mary Randle, Mrs Roberts, Mrs Rook, Mrs Sly, Albert Squires, Mrs Squires, Phyllis Squires, Mrs Winwood. The parents and grandparents of Mrs Williams of Trimpley, who provided this photograph, are among the group. *(Mrs D.E. Williams)*

12 May for Kenneth Haycock and Kenneth Cooke of Peel Street, and Charlie Brooks, youngest son of John Brooks and his late wife of 3 The Serpentine, Sutton Farm Estate. Charlie had arrived home on 26 April after being imprisoned in Germany for five years. He was forced to march 800 miles by his captors in an attempt to stop him and his fellow prisoners being rescued by the Allies. The British 2nd Army eventually rescued them at Ilsen.'

There was also a party at the Royal George, Hall Street, held for Pte Sidney Reading, son of Mr and Mrs C. Reading of 15 Dudley Street. Sidney had also been a prisoner for five years.

These are just three of the many parties that took place for returning service people, not only in Kidderminster, but also all over the country. Joyous occasions they must have been for parents and families welcoming home their loved ones.

12

SUNDRY REMINISCENCES

Many people, all but two of whom wish to remain anonymous, remember particular aspects or stories about the war which made an impression on them. Some are reproduced below:

A sunny day, 3 September 1939. Picture me, aged four and a half, curly fair hair tied up with ribbons dressed in my favourite Anniversary Dress of pale blue organdie (Mother thought I was the next Shirley Temple). My coat was of deep forget-me-not blue, velvet on the collar and pockets like those worn by Princess Margaret Rose. My auntie in London bought it for me.

We used to go to The New Church on Comberton Hill, some two and a half miles from our home in Bruce Road. I had been there that morning with my father and brother Norman, and was skipping home as carefree as a lark. My dad was impatient and almost cross with me as I jumped and skipped and sang. In retrospect, he knew something we did not. As we came down the Birmingham Road, past Sheward's fields – where the Cairndhu estate now stands – I was urged to hurry and went sprawling. The footpath had new tarmac so my coat, dress and face were splattered with tar; and I had a great, bleeding, hole in my knee. The toes of my black patent shoes were scraped off and I was terrified at the thought of my mother's wrath. So I was dragged home yelling; but when we got there no one noticed my state. My mother was in the kitchen weeping and made the amazing statement: 'We are at war with Germany. You'll have to go and fight!'

Norman and I shot out to the front gate, fully expecting to see our soldiers in red coats and bearskin hats, fighting with German soldiers. Of course, no one was there. The sleepy road was empty, the sun shone, and there was an eerie silence.

So I was saved from my mother's wrath by the outbreak of war! Even when Mum finally noticed my state, she was too distracted to say much. Years later, of course, I realised that for my parents' generation, memories of the Great War were all too close.

Pieces of shrapnel collected in Kidderminster.
(John Russell)

I still have the shrapnel collected by my father during the war. It's going rusty after all these years but I don't really like to get rid of it. *(John Russell)*

It was difficult to get around in the war if you weren't local. Road signs and town names were removed to confuse the enemy should they invade. Railway signs were painted over and, if you were lucky enough to be able to travel out of your area, you had to know where you were going.

In the war there was no opportunity to modernise houses and we had no running water. On Areley Common there was one pump to serve four houses and we had to boil the kettle for hot water. My mother didn't go out to work so in order to earn a little money my mother used to do her brother's and sister's washing using a dolly tub.

There was so little traffic in our village that the lads could play on the road. Most of the transport locally was by horse. I remember the muck cart coming round to empty the bucket toilets – we didn't have flush lavatories then. It was pulled by an old horse which seemed to be in a permanent daze. I think he was anaesthetised by the smell.

Where the Stourport Job Centre is now Jack Jones kept a market selling corn and seeds. He had a pony and trap and delivered bran for fowls. We would run out and ask him if we could have a ride on his cart. He would take us round the town and although he made a lot of deliveries he never spoke to the pony once. He just whistled and the pony knew exactly what to do.

Prices in the war were low by today's standards and there was no real inflation. Cherries were 1s 6d a bag throughout the war. Cream cakes from Ferris's cake shop were a rarity and people needed to queue for them at 7 for 6d. A hot loaf from Tubbs the bakers was tuppence farthing and beer was one shilling a pint. However the breweries couldn't cope with the demand for beer so its alcohol content was 'reduced'; this was sold more cheaply at 10d a pint.

I remember the information given out at cinemas telling you what to do in the event of a gas attack – hang wet sheets and towels round the doors and windows. I was anxious about this and asked my mother what we should do. 'Don't worry,' she said. 'I won't let it come in here.' I was happy with that!

The government issued leaflets to make the public aware of various hazards that they might face. One of these described what anti-personnel bombs looked like. (See overleaf.)

My father was a guard on the GWR [Great Western Railway] and worked the line from Kidderminster to Ditton Priors. He told me that one day he was coming over Far Forest when the engine coupling broke loose. He was left in charge of a train of thirty-two wagons full of 18-inch naval shells running back down the track towards Bewdley. There were thirty shells in each wagon. He, as the brakeman, had to try and stop them. He clambered along the top of the wagons to each brake and managed to stop the train at Northwood Halt.

The shells weren't primed but a big enough impact could have set them off. There would have been massive damage if the shells had exploded. The story was kept top-secret. He didn't talk about it much – possibly because one of his duties was to ensure that the train was properly coupled. The engine driver

DANGER

SMALL ANTI-PERSONNEL BOMB

BEWARE OF THESE BOMBS WHICH ARE VERY
DESTRUCTIVE AND ARE MEANT TO DO YOU HARM.

THEY MAY BE FOUND

—   LIKE THIS   —   OR   —   LIKE THIS   —

BOMB WITH CASING OPEN   BOMB WITH CASING CLOSED

**IF YOU SEE THEM DO NOT TOUCH, KEEP AWAY
AND REPORT THEM TO THE WARDENS OR POLICE**

**DO NOT TOUCH SUSPICIOUS OBJECTS
REPORT THEM TO WARDENS OR POLICE**

Issued by the Ministry of Home Security

1/43 (15037) 21082/321 50,000 7/43 K.H.K. Gp. 8/8

Leaflet warning of danger
from anti-personnel bombs.
(John Russell)

didn't stop; he probably made sure he was as far away as possible when he
discovered the wagons had run back.

There were few cars in those days and petrol was rationed. Dad's only form of
transport was a black sit-up-and-beg bicycle with a home-made wooden saddle
on the crossbar for me to ride on. My mother and elder brother had their own
bikes and we cycled everywhere. It was not unusual to ride from Kidderminster
to Doverdale Church to lay flowers on the grave of my mother's parents. My
Aunt Lucy was the landlady of the nearby Ripperidge Inn, which in those days
was a 'men-only' alehouse as well as being a smallholding farm. They made
their own cider from apples grown locally and pressed in the yard. The beer
was kept in barrels at the back in a cool building and served from a jug. My
uncles Jack and Ted Lamb served wearing aprons and a towel over their arms.
Most customers were farmers or farm workers. When we visited we took our

own sandwiches and sat outside drinking lemonade. Only my dad was allowed in the bar.

Our church was Baptist and in case of fire the baptistry was kept full of water. For security reasons we had to turn off the electricity at the mains switch near the front door of the church – so you had to go through the church to get to it. Once one of the lads, Les Arnold, was showing off his new raincoat. New clothes were very rare and he was swanking about it. He volunteered to go and turn the electricity off and this plunged the church into pitch darkness. Walking back through the church he fell into the baptistry and was absolutely soaked. We said, 'That new raincoat's not very good at keeping you dry, is it?'

So many things have changed. For example Brintons had a sports ground at Spennells. There was a swimming pool, diving board, changing rooms, tennis courts, cricket and soccer pitches. It was very active in the war and lots of people used it. They had a big three-storey clubhouse, like a manor house. After the war Barnardos moved in, knocked it down and built a new house – with a house mother for the children in each wing.

My dad and Mary Seager's were Special Constables who patrolled a circular route round the village. On some occasions they would have to meet at the end of the Common and they did that by patrolling in opposite directions. On one night it was so dark in the blackout that neither realised that the other had arrived; they stood either side of a tree for ages until one of them moved.

We made a lot of our own entertainment as children. We used to play a game at Stourport station: we would run to the top of the footbridge and when the train came the girls would lift their skirts and the boys their trousers so that the steam could run up our legs.

In wartime materials were scarce and it was always 'make do and mend'. I recall my mother darning our socks, using what looked like a wooden toadstool, and it was not unusual to cover the frayed ends of jacket sleeves with leather. My dad used bits from the carpet industry: my shoes were repaired with leather cut from old picking straps off Wilton looms. My mother knitted me a long-sleeved pullover from carpet yarn! After several washings and passages through the mangle, it was still stiff and 'itchy', although I did wear it to play in.

There was little traffic during the Second World War and we could play out in the Lane quite safely: rounders, tick, tracking, hopscotch, cricket, sledging in the winter and many other childhood pastimes. Sometimes a game needed someone to be 'on' – someone to start the activity. To choose this person we would gather together in a circle and the senior child would point successively at each individual reciting to the rhythm of the accented chant:

> Eeney Meeney Mac a Rac a Dare Eye
> Dum a Rac, a Chick a Pock, a Lollipop
> a Rum – Tum – Push.

The child who finished up with a 'Push' was 'on'. It was only after I had become one of the older children that I realised that it was easy to fix who was to be chosen by knowing where to start in the circle.

When some of us Pay Corps girls had been out for a few drinks on our way back to our billets we would mix up fire watching notices for a joke. The Fire Watchers had a message fastened to the front of their houses telling them when to report for duty. We thought it was quite funny to swap them round.

All over the country round concrete blocks were placed at strategic sites so that they could be rolled into positions on roads to inhibit the passage of armoured vehicles in case of invasion. Some of those blocks have found a use as bollards near the dodgems in the fairground at Stourport.

At the bottom of Sutton Park Road, opposite Holy Innocents Church, there was a bit of spare land. On this was built a six-sided brick box. It had an entry

Concrete blocks at Stourport Fairground, once part of the road blockade defence system instituted to combat possible invasion. *(Bob Millward)*

on one side and gaps instead of windows on the remaining sides. It was probably what was called a pillbox. I was told it was to be used by troops or civilians with rifles if we were invaded.

There was a constant fear of invasion – particularly parachutists. For a joke, boys at the Grammar School would stop what they were doing and gaze skywards. Soon a whole crowd would gather round – looking at nothing!

I vividly remember being sent to the isolation hospital in Birmingham on 6 February 1941. At a time when children from Birmingham were being evacuated to Kidderminster I was sent into the thick of the bombing. I had scarlet fever, was 6 years old and terrified. My father managed to get me some peppermint creams before I went – hardly invalid fare but at least they were something to suck.

The ambulance took me to Hayley Green Isolation Hospital – on my own. No parents were allowed. At the hospital I was enclosed in a bedroom with sheets at the door soaked in something smelly. For some while I was too ill to notice much but I was aware of the night-time bombardment going on all around. There were no blinds at the windows and you could see the searchlights sweeping the sky, and hear the sirens, the drone of planes, booming crashes and crumps of bombs and terrified children crying for their mums. The nurses responded with: 'Stop crying or Hitler will get you.' Real tender loving care!

I was there for six weeks. When I got home, thin and hardly able to stand, my auntie visited bringing a bag of oranges and some chocolate. Whilst she nattered to my mother they forgot me as I sat under the table and munched my way through some oranges and the chocolate – until I was spectacularly and violently sick! Mother said later, 'Do you remember those little parcels I sent you every week when you were at Hayley Green? All the neighbours gave up their sweet and chocolate rations for you.' I never saw any of it – not a taste. Ah me, my mum was so upset.

Towards the end of the war a German plane was put on display in the cattle market, Market Street. I don't know where it had been brought down. It was pale blue and I think it was a Messerschmitt.

There was a significant and welcome military presence in Kidderminster during the Second World War, but one military force that would not have been embraced would have been invading Germans. Nevertheless, Kidderminster had prepared for that eventuality and a crudely prepared hand-typed advice leaflet was issued in March 1943 with the title *If We Are Invaded*.

The Mayor Lou Tolley wrote in the foreword: 'Although invasion by the enemy may seem remote at the moment no one can say what will happen before the war ends, and it is better to be prepared for any eventuality than to be found wanting in essential matters.'

The leaflet deals with where people made homeless should go; what to do if water and sanitation facilities are disrupted; and where to get news. Emergency food centres would be set up in the Brinton Park tea room, Franche School, St Oswald's Hall (Broadwaters), Milton Hall (Lorne Street), Bennett Street School, Coventry Street School and the Cattle Market. Fortunately, the contents of this leaflet proved superfluous to our needs.

Bricked up within the sandstone rock at the rear of Margaret Thatcher House, Mill Street, is the air-raid shelter used by inhabitants of Mill Street and Mill Lane during the Second World War. Access was via The Gully and the Forty-Eight Steps, each leading from Mill Lane. Both step-ways still exist today.

Italian prisoners of war could be found in Todd's Yard, Mill Lane. Most were friendly and talked to locals from the perimeter wall. During the day they were taken to work on farms or other labouring activities. After the war many remained in Britain and married English girls. I remember one prisoner making me a signet ring from, I believe, a penny coin. It was decorated with 'J' for my name, Judy, and this poem commemorates that event.

The Prisoner's Gift

In the year of nineteen forty four
With dear old England still at war,
A prisoner from sunny Italy
Over the camp wall beckoned to me,
He smiled and then held out his hand
Within the palm lay a small gold band,
A signet ring he'd made for me
The letter 'J' I could plainly see.
How many hours had he patiently spent?
How many memories into it went?
Tender thought of a girl and home
Perhaps a little child of his own.
His kindly gift meant so much to me,
From a man whose hope was 'Liberty'.

Judy George

Near the end of the war I went on holiday with a friend to her sister's home in Glyn Neath, South Wales. Holidays were quite a thing then. I remember sitting in that cottage and hearing the announcement that an atom bomb had been dropped on Japan. I can hear him now, and remember saying: 'What on earth's an atom bomb?' Then they talked about a huge mushroom of smoke clouds. We couldn't begin to understand what they were talking about. Within days the second one was dropped and Japan surrendered. And that was the real end of the war.

BIBLIOGRAPHY

Primary sources

Kidderminster Library, Minutes of the Kidderminster Town Council 1939–1946
—— *Kidderminster Shuttle and Stourport Courier* (on microfilm)
The Carpet Museum, Kidderminster, Archive Collection, *A Record of War Production, Brintons Ltd, Kidderminster and Bridgwater 1939–1945*
Worcester Record Office, Spetchley, The Log Books of St George's Infant and Junior Schools, Kidderminster

Secondary sources

Barrie, Doris, Caswell, Betty, and Mathews, Roger, *Journal of the Wolverley and Cookley Historical Society*, vol 11, p. 65, 2001. Available at most Wyre Forest Libraries and the Society headquarters, The Parish Hall, Wolverley

Birt, David, *The Battle of Bewdley*, Bewdley, Peter Huxtable Designs, 1988

Bryant, Sheila (compiler), *Memories of Wartime Evacuation 1939–1946*, Smethwick Heritage Centre Trust, 2001

Creaton, Heather J., *Sources for the History of London 1939–45: A Guide and Bibliography*, British Records Association, 1998 (consulted via Internet)

Dickson, Sally, Elliott, Bill, and Warner, Richard (eds), *Recollections of Childhood in Kidderminster*, Kidderminster & District Archaeological & Historical Society, 1993

Gilbert, Nigel, *Kidderminster Foreign – Portraits of Trimpley and Habberley*, Kidderminster, Kidderminster Foreign Parish Council, 2002

Park, Betty, *Horsefair and Broadwaters – Born to the Manor*, Bewdley, Bewdley Historical Research Group, 2003

Ramsey, Winston G. (ed), *The Blitz – Then And Now*, vols 1–3, London, Battle of Britain Prints International Ltd, 1987–1990

Tomkinson, Ken and Hall, George, *Kidderminster Since 1800*, Kidderminster, published by the authors, 1975